LIFE IN ORGANIZATIONS

PARADOXES, DILEMMAS AND POSSIBILITIES

PRASAD KURIAN

INDIA • SINGAPORE • MALAYSIA

Notion Press

No.8, 3rd Cross Street,
CIT Colony, Mylapore,
Chennai, Tamil Nadu – 600004

First Published by Notion Press 2021
Copyright © Prasad Kurian 2021
All Rights Reserved.

ISBN 978-1-63781-617-2

This book has been published with all efforts taken to make the material error-free after the consent of the author. However, the author and the publisher do not assume and hereby disclaim any liability to any party for any loss, damage, or disruption caused by errors or omissions, whether such errors or omissions result from negligence, accident, or any other cause.

While every effort has been made to avoid any mistake or omission, this publication is being sold on the condition and understanding that neither the author nor the publishers or printers would be liable in any manner to any person by reason of any mistake or omission in this publication or for any action taken or omitted to be taken or advice rendered or accepted on the basis of this work. For any defect in printing or binding the publishers will be liable only to replace the defective copy by another copy of this work then available.

This book is dedicated to

My mentors
for encouraging me to look at life in organizations with new eyes

My family
for embracing me with all my paradoxes and possibilities

CONTENTS

	Preface	7
Chapter 1:	Introducing paradoxes, dilemmas and life in organizations	9
Chapter 2:	Paradoxes in entering the organization	14
Chapter 3:	Paradoxes in performance and effectiveness	21
Chapter 4:	Paradoxes in learning and capability building	36
Chapter 5:	Paradoxes in careers and career planning	52
Chapter 6:	Paradoxes in rewards and recognition	63
Chapter 7:	Paradoxes in engagement, belonging and identity	86
Chapter 8:	Paradoxes in the big picture - vision, mission, values and change	106
Chapter 9:	Paradoxes in leadership and followership	118
Chapter 10:	Paradoxes in leaving the organization	130
Chapter 11:	Embracing the paradoxes and the possibilities	138

PREFACE

I started my career as a Scientist Engineer at the Vikram Sarabhai Space Centre of the Indian Space Research Organization. Engineering is essentially about problem solving. Yes, it also involves creativity, optimising within constraints and making design trade-offs. However, the core reality remains that the problems in engineering are meant to be solved. After I made the 'quantum jump' from engineering to management, I started becoming more aware of another type of 'problems' – problems that cannot be, and even should not be, 'solved' in the engineering sense.

Perhaps, I got the first glimpse of these type of 'problems' while I was studying at XLRI Jamshedpur for my MBA. One my elective courses was on 'Applied Psychoanalysis'. A case study, that we attempted as part of that course, dealt with a woman who exhibited inconsistent or even contradictory patterns of behavior. In some situations, she behaved in a 'virtuous' manner, and, in some other situations she behaved in an 'immoral' manner. We were split into subgroups and we were asked to reach a consensus and make a presentation in 45 minutes' time on whether she was 'virtuous' or 'immoral'. Our subgroup jumped right into the discussion. However, our discussion was not being conclusive, with some of the team members arguing for one position and the others for the opposite position.

While most of us were enjoying the discussion, one of my friends, who was the most sincere and result-oriented among us, was getting increasingly uneasy because we were nearing the time-limit set by the professor while being nowhere near any consensus. Finally, he could take it no more and he said "OK, OK, let us agree that she is 70 percent virtuous and 30 percent immoral". There was indeed some 'logical' merit in this solution', because if we looked at each of the incidents described in the case, classified her behavior in each of them as 'good' or 'bad' we would come to this answer mathematically. However, in a way, this answer completely missed the point. The 'real purpose' of assigning this case to us, though it was not stated explicitly when we were given the case, was not to solve it. The real purpose was to develop our awareness of the paradoxical nature of the issue, and to become aware of the tendency to classify women as either 'virtuous' or 'immoral'. Therefore, the solution was to grapple with the problem unsuccessfully and from that struggle reach a higher level of awareness, understanding and appreciation!

As I started working in the management domain, initially as a management consultant and then as an employee, I began to encounter these kinds of situations more and more in various contexts. Slowly, it occurred to me that these kinds of paradoxical situations are probably the norm, as opposed to being exceptions, when it comes to life in business organizations, especially in matters related to people and people management. This book is the outcome of my struggle with these paradoxes, contradictions and dilemmas over the last two decades. While this struggle can indeed be very frustrating, it also holds the key to achieve a higher level of awareness and more nuanced understanding that can open a wide range of possibilities for us – possibilities for responding creatively and effectively to the paradoxical situations that we face at work and in life.

In this book, I invite you come with me on a journey through the paradoxes, dilemmas, polarities and possibilities in the various aspects of organizational life. Our focus will be on 'real world paradoxes' that impact our effectiveness in business organizations, as opposed to 'logical paradoxes' that are more like logical riddles. The plan is to organize this journey in a manner that anyone who works in business organizations should find it interesting. If you are a people manager or a business leader or if you work in the Human Resources domain you will find many additional insights. I do not promise any algorithmic solutions or to do lists. However, I do promise a lot of triggers for insights!

CHAPTER 1: INTRODUCING PARADOXES, DILEMMAS AND LIFE IN ORGANIZATIONS

"When I use a word", Humpty Dumpty said in rather a scornful tone, "it means just what I choose it to mean - neither more nor less".

-Lewis Carroll, Through the Looking Glass

Since we are not living in the Wonderland of Alice and Humpty Dumpty, let us begin our journey by taking a closer look at some of the key words that we will be encountering in this journey. This is important as words like paradox and dilemma can mean different things in different contexts. We are not attempting formal or universally accepted definitions here. Our effort is just to develop some tentative operational definitions that will help us in developing a shared understanding, for the purpose of our journey here.

Life in organizations

When we use the phrase, 'life in organizations' or 'organizational life' we are primarily referring to the experience of the employees in business organizations. It also refers to the experience of the people who attempt to 'manage' the employees in some way, like people managers, business leaders and Human Resources (HR) professionals. Our attempt will be to look at the key situations and aspects that impact employee experience from the perspectives of the various stakeholders.

Paradoxes, dilemmas, polarities and dialectics

A paradox is a situation with an inherent contradiction. A paradox occurs when there are multiple points of view on an issue, each of which are true and essential, but they appear to be in conflict with one another. This implies that that we cannot resolve a paradox in the way we solve a typical problem. We cannot choose one of the options over the others without oversimplifying the situation. What is possible is to struggle with the paradoxical situation for a sufficient period of time so that we can reach a higher level of awareness and deeper understanding of the context and the issue, that will enable us to come up with the most effective response at a given moment. These responses are not necessarily solutions in the normal sense of the word 'solution'. Sometimes, these are effective ways of coping with the situation. Sometimes, these responses involve totally reframing the situation and opening up radically new possibilities.

Here, we are using the term paradox and paradoxical thinking in a broad manner. Therefore, it will also involve dilemmas, polarities and dialectic, though strictly speaking, they are not necessarily paradoxes. A dilemma occurs when one has to make a choice between two mutually exclusive options, neither of which is clearly better than the other one. If these options are polar opposites, then we have a polarity. A dialectic is a pattern that begins with a thesis followed by an antithesis and resolved by a higher synthesis. This synthesis can be followed by another antithesis and the pattern can repeat, though at a higher level, as one point of view teaches the other point of view instead of invalidating it! Another term that is relevant to our journey is irony. Irony occurs when what actually happens turns out to be completely different from what was expected. In a way, irony is the paradox of consequences.

Not all the problems that we face in organizational life are paradoxes. Many of the problems that we find in organizational life can be solved using regular problem-solving methods. Categorizing a simple problem as a paradox can complicate our lives unnecessarily. Some problems are to be solved, some problems are to be swamped out by putting them in the broader context and some problems are to be approached through paradoxical thinking. Our exploration here will put us in a better position to correctly identify and respond to paradoxical situations.

Responding to the paradoxes in organizational life

The 'ideal' way to respond to paradoxes is to use the 'both-and' approach instead of the 'either-or' approach when it comes to choosing between the options. The basic concept here is to look at the options or poles as inseparable or independent, somewhat like the two faces of a coin. While this approach of replacing the 'tyranny of the OR' with the 'magic of the AND' looks great, it might not always be practically feasible. While the focus on synergy over trade-offs seems attractive, it often comes at the risk of oversimplifying the situation and that of emptying paradox of its emergent, surprising, and often uncontrollable effects. Therefore, there is no getting away from the necessary struggle with the paradox and gaining wisdom from the same.

Yes, understanding and experiencing the dynamic interplay between the opposite poles is the essential first step in dealing with paradoxes, dilemmas and polarities. In addition to helping us find the appropriate dynamic equilibrium among the opposing forces, this can also be a trigger for coming up with creative, effective and sustainable responses to the paradoxical situation. We can also look at these approaches to dealing with paradoxes as possibilities that we can configure in appropriate ways depending on what will be most relevant in a specific context.

The use of Irony can be a great tool to understand and to cope with paradoxes. Irony can make the underlying meanings visible through humour. The use of irony enables us to express our struggles with the contradictions at the workplace in a positive manner, and to put them in the larger paradoxical context. This gives us a head start in our endeavour to come up with creative responses to the paradoxes, dilemmas and polarities that we face in organizational life.

Simplicity on the other side of complexity

Responding effectively to paradoxes is like finding the simplicity on the other side of complexity. There are simplicities on both the sides of complexity. The simplicity on this side of complexity is deceptive and ineffective, because it comes from oversimplification or ignoring the complexity of the situation. It is just simplistic. However, there is another type of simplicity that one can arrive at by working through the complexity. This is a profound kind of simplicity, and, responses to the situation from this simplicity are wise and effective. The paradoxical thinking that we are looking at in this journey is an attempt to reach this simplicity on the other side of complexity. This opens up new perspectives and new possibilities for us.

Roadmap for the rest of our journey

Paradox is a central dimension of life in organizations. Decision-making in organizations is becoming increasingly paradoxical with the increasing amount of uncertainty in the environment, shifting priorities and goalposts and conflicting objectives. We constantly need to deal with the tensions between the old and the new, between the individual and the collective, between process focus and flexibility, between performance and development, between efficiency and agility, between internal demands and external demands etc. They create stress, discomfort and anxiety in us. This is especially true in the field of people management. This should not be surprising. Being human is essentially about being free, spontaneous and authentic. The term management, in the traditional sense of planning and controlling, does not fit well with the humanness of the employees. We often see the most innovative people becoming the least innovative employees. We find it difficult to bring who we are into what we do. Work life can become more about impressing others as opposed to expressing oneself. Paradoxical thinking can be a great tool for us in organizational life, as it can help us to be more effective and fulfilled as employees, people managers and as human resources professionals.

In the chapters that follow, we will look at the various paradoxical aspects of life in business organizations. In many of these cases, I became aware of the paradoxical nature of the situation based on actual conversations or incidents that I came across. In order to give you a first-hand feel, I have retained these conversations, while maintaining the anonymity of the people and organizations involved. Hence, you will find that many of the sub-sections in this book start with the record of a conversation.

In all these cases, the attempt will be to highlight the multiple perspectives and opinions on the situation that are often in conflict with one another and thereby creating a paradox. We will look at them closely and wrestle with the contradictions for a while to develop a deeper understanding and appreciation. We will also see pointers on some of the possibilities that can trigger our thinking so that we can come up with creative responses that are appropriate to the specific contexts that we find ourselves in. In the concluding chapter of this book, we will consolidate the learnings from our journey through the paradoxes and possibilities in the various aspects of organizational life so that it will serve as a ready reckoner for embracing the paradoxes and possibilities!

Let us begin our exploration!

CHAPTER 2: PARADOXES IN ENTERING THE ORGANIZATION

"Begin at the beginning", the King said, very gravely, "and go on till you come to the end: then stop".

-Lewis Carroll, Alice in Wonderland

Therefore, let us begin at the beginning, by looking at the paradoxes involved in joining an organization and in hiring people into an organization.

From the employee point of view, there are multiple perspectives on what are the factors that one should look at in deciding which organization to join. For example, should one give more importance to the job content, salary, culture, capability and career development opportunities, work life balance, reputation of the reporting manager, company brand or the employer brand? Should one look at the new organization as a stepping-stone, as a career enhancer or as the career destination?

From the organization and hiring manager point of view also there are multiple perspectives on what should be given higher importance while making a selection decision. For example, should the organization prioritize the functional, technical or the behavioral competencies? How much importance should be given to the 'person-organization fit' as compared to 'person-job fit'? Should a 'safe candidate' with proven credentials be preferred over someone who brings in a different dimension with the associated risks and opportunities?

All these are paradoxes that defy algorithmic solutions and standard responses. Hence, what we can do is to make an extra effort to understand the organisation context, the various factors driving the selection decisions, the options and the consequences of the options, and come up with a decision that is most appropriate to the current context. For example, in the current context, is the ability to drive transformation more important than the ability to maintain stability? Alternatively, from the point of view of the employee, which factor should be given more importance at this point considering the larger life and career context of the employee? Yes, if we wrestle with these paradoxes long enough, better solutions that integrate multiple priorities in an innovative manner are likely to evolve.

Let us look at a couple of paradoxical aspects, that are foundational to this domain, in more detail; one mainly from the organisation point of view and the next mainly from the employee point of view. We will also look at the issue of whether age of the candidate could be a factor in hiring decisions.

The paradox of hiring great people and letting them decide

There is one particular approach to hiring that that I find to be particularly interesting. It goes something like this: "Hire good people and empower them to decide what is to be done and how it is to be done". The basic idea here is that in a complex and rapidly changing environment, the traditional approach of specifying (to each employee) what exactly has to be done is unlikely to work. Therefore, it is better to hire good people and let them figure out what needs to be done.

I am not saying that this approach is 'wrong'. My point is just that there is a paradox here. In order to hire 'good' people, the organization has to use some definition for 'good', a 'working definition' of what 'good' means in their context, so that it can be used in the hiring process as the selection criteria. After all, one cannot do hiring without some sort of criteria, implicit or explicit. This leads to an interesting situation. This definition of 'good' is coloured by the current thinking in the organization. To put it in another way, the criteria gets influenced by the organization's (often implicit) understanding of what is required to be done, how it should be done and hence what sort of a person can do it. Therefore, the current thinking in the organization with its associated limitations gets built into the hiring criteria inadvertently.

Let us look at the most common example of this situation. Organization 'A' is in trouble. The organization does not have a clear understanding of what is to be done to get out of this situation. Therefore, it decides to hire a 'good' CEO and let him figure out what needs to be done. However, when the organization chooses a 'good CEO' that choice is coloured by the stated or unstated definition of 'a good CEO,' which in turn is limited by the current thinking or consciousness in the organization.

This can be addressed to some extent by looking at 'best practices' (what has worked in CEO selection elsewhere in similar situations) and by using external advisers. But this might not always work as the uniqueness of that particular organization context might get missed out and also because the external advice and best practice information often goes through one level of processing or filtering within the organization (when decision-making is done by existing people), which in turn brings in the limitations of the current thinking in the organization.

Hence, the approach of 'hiring good people and letting them figure out what needs to be done' might not be as simple as it appears to be!

Polarities of 'what good looks like'

In my career, I have had the good fortune of experiencing many organization contexts, both as an external consultant and as an employee. Based on these experiences, I have come to realize that organizations often have different definitions of the 'picture of success at an individual level' (that is, what good individual performance looks like). While the tasks will vary from one job to the other within the organization, there are common patterns that hold good across jobs in an organization on what good performance (or 'excellence' or 'quality') looks like. However, these patterns can vary a lot from one organization to the other. When people move from one organization to the other, this can create rude shocks, for both the employee and the organization, especially when an employee who has been successful in one organization joins another organization that has a different definition of excellence ('what good looks like').

Let us take a closer look at these underlying (tacit) definitions of quality (or excellence). While each organization has its own underlying definition (assumption), it can be useful to conceptualize these underlying assumptions as points in a continuum between two polar opposites: 'absence of variation' and 'presence of value'.

At one end, we have organizations where the underlying definition of quality is very much similar to the 'six sigma definition' - 'the absence of variation'. In these organizations, the performance of an employee considered to be the excellent, if he thinks through the goals before agreeing to the same, creates a detailed plan to work towards the goals in a systematic manner and archives goals even when there were changes in the environment. These organizations also tend to value and invest in building capability or expertise, at both people and process levels. Hence, the premium is on good design, deep expertise, meticulous planning, reliability, consistency, coherence and congruence. In extreme cases, this can lead to rigidity.

At the other end of the continuum, we have organizations where the definition is more like 'the presence of value' or 'the fitness for purpose'. Here the focus is on 'trial and error'. Simply put, the underlying message is that 'do whatever makes most sense in a particular situation'. In these organizations, muddling through things is acceptable and even preferred (instead of thinking through things and seeking clarity before starting the work). People who insist on planning and consistency are considered to be 'risk-averse' or even to be 'lacking in courage'. Operating with contradictions and the lack of consistency are considered to be 'heroic'. A lot of emphasis is placed on pragmatism (as opposed to expertise) and on workarounds. Hence, the premium is on 'flexibility' and 'crisis handling'. In extreme cases, it can lead to an organization that jumps from one idea (or goal or fad) to another on a frequent basis.

There is nothing inherently 'good' or 'bad' about these underlying definitions - they are just different (equally valid) ways of looking at the world. The point is that these variations exist across organizations and it could have a significant bearing on employee performance, engagement and retention.

To some extent, these assumptions are related to the environment in which the organization is operating in. But it is often it is a matter of the preferred way of responding to the environment. These assumptions are also closely related to the culture of the organization, especially the deeper levels of culture – like the values and the basic underlying assumptions.

This brings us to the question of adaptation. Employees can adjust. Organizations can change too, though usually it is a very slow process and require a critical mass of new employees with new preferences. The individual's definition of 'good' can also change. However, the individual's definition of 'good' is shaped mainly by his personality and his 'early career experiences', and, a change in the same requires lot of time and a critical mass of high impact (profound or traumatic) new experiences. Hence, for the time being, let us focus on the issue of new employees attempting to align with the organization's definition of 'good performance'.

Yes, employees do realize that they are unlikely to find an organization that provides a perfect match and that they need to adjust. However, if an employee needs to constantly act outside his preferences, it can lead to stress. This can also lead to mediocrity as the individuals are not able to play to their strengths. Excellence and engagement at individual level requires the opportunity 'to bring more of who you are into what you do'. It is critical for those employees who look at work as one of the avenues for self-expression. Similarly, when organizations talk about connecting with employees at higher levels of the 'needs hierarchy', this becomes important for the organizations also.

One of my all-time favourite books is 'Zen and the Art of Motorcycle Maintenance' by Robert M. Pirsig. This book begins with the following lines: "And what is good, Phaedrus, And what is not good, Need we ask anyone to tell us these things?". In the context of our discussion here (for a person who is trying to join a new organization or for an organization trying to hire someone), the answer should be a loud 'Yes'. It is definitely worthwhile to ask this explicitly, listen carefully, 'read' between the lines and to be very careful about what is left unsaid!

When age is not just a number!

Let us begin by looking at a couple of statements that I heard that made me think more about this aspect.

"Though it is not written in the job specifications, we have been asked by the client to look for a candidate below 45 years of age for the CHRO role", said the executive search consultant who was asking for a reference.

"We decided to make the job offer to this particular candidate mainly because she was younger as compared to the other equally good candidates. We wanted to hire someone who can be developed into more senior level leadership roles. We want to be able to see the 'next to next role' for the candidate before we make a hiring decision", said the business leader.

These days, it not so rare to come across statements like these. They make me wonder if they demonstrate some sort of 'ageism' at the workplace or if there are other more 'rational' reasons involved! Is age the issue or is it being used as a convenient 'proxy' for other factors?

The typical 'reasons' why someone comes up with a statement like the first one (the one made by the executive search consultant) include things like 'decision to bring in younger candidates at the CXO level as part of a business transformation exercise', 'the other CXOs being in the same age bracket', 'a workforce that is predominantly Gen Y', 'the need to bring in fresh thinking at senior levels' etc. It is true that the experience range specified for many roles is coming down. Now there is a greater emphasis on learning agility as opposed to experience. Also, knowledge goes out of shape and can be acquired much faster these days. It is also possible that the older (more experienced) candidates are just more expensive. Yes, there could also be cases where long years of experience is assumed to create some sort of rigidity and lack of flexibility, lack of appetite for risk taking, lack of creativity or lack of tech-savviness.

One is more likely to come across statements similar to the second one (the one made by the business leader) in Multi-National Companies. Having greater runway left for the career is valued especially in those cases where there is a fixed retirement age. Yes, there are still some traditional companies where higher number of years of experience is an advantage. This brings up an interesting question: Isn't the very concept of a 'mandatory retirement age' a clear sign of ageism?

In domains like HR, there is an even more basic question that we need to look at: "Do organizations have many HR jobs that would require a level of expertise which would take more than 20 years to develop?". If the answer is "No", then it creates a fundamental problem for the HR professionals who are in the 'more than 20 years' experience range. In addition to the basic aspect of finding employment, if one is also concerned about the aspect of finding enriching and meaningful work, the problem gets even more challenging.

I do wonder what this means for the mid-career professionals in all functions. There is always the risk that one can get replaced with someone who is more in line with the evolving requirement of the job and/or is at a lower cost. The ideal response to this kind of a problem is that one constantly learns to keep the skill set relevant, takes up roles of increasing responsibility where the experience adds value, and ensures that one's contribution to the organization is much higher than one's salary cost. But this is easier said than done!

We do see an increasing number of mid-career professionals taking up consulting or freelancing kind of options. The trouble is just that majority of those mid-career professionals are unlikely to earn at least as much as they were earning in their regular job. Yes, there are a few who make it really big. There are also quite a few who use this opportunity to reinvent themselves and configure some sort of 'portfolio life and career' that is more aligned to their higher calling or more conducive to their self-actualization journey. So, there are many possibilities, though all of them require a lot of effort!

CHAPTER 3: PARADOXES IN PERFORMANCE AND EFFECTIVENESS

"My dear, here we must run as fast as we can, just to stay in place. And, if you wish to go anywhere you must run twice as fast as that".

-Lewis Carroll, Alice in Wonderland

Making progress in business organizations can indeed feel like running on a treadmill. In this chapter, let us look at the important aspect of doing well and getting things done in organizations. Here also, there are no shortages of paradoxes, both from the employer and the employee point of view.

For example, should the performance goals for the employees be defined at the beginning of the year or should the performance be managed more fluidly through regular conversations? Should the organization use performance ratings, and if yes, should the ratings be normalized? If an organization moves away from the use of performance ratings, how will it link performance and rewards in an objective manner? Should the organization give more importance to short-term performance or to long-term performance of the employees? Similarly, how much relative importance should the employee give to maximising performance as compared to focusing on skill-building? Does the answer change, if the organization has a 'hire and fire' track record? Should the employee put work-life balance above job performance?

Now, let take a closer look at some of the paradoxical situations related to performance. We will also examine if there is really something like a 'high-performance' culture. Finally, we will look at the need to rethink performance management, keeping in mind the paradoxical nature of the domain.

Performance ratings and the 'above average effect'

Have you ever wondered why the sharing of performance ratings is often an unpleasant experience, both for the employees and for the managers of the employees?

There could be many reasons for this. The performance objectives and targets might not have been properly defined or agreed upon. There might have been changes in the context or factors outside the employee's control that made the targets impossible to achieve. The performance feedback might not have been given regularly and accurately (managers often try to 'soften' negative feedback) and hence the rating might have come as a surprise to the employee. However, I feel that most of the unpleasantness of the situation is related to a psychological phenomenon known as 'superiority illusion' or the 'above average effect'.

'Illusory superiority' is a cognitive bias that causes people to overestimate their positive qualities and abilities and to underestimate their negative qualities, relative to others. This manifests in a wide range of areas including intelligence, possession of desirable characteristics, performance on tests and of course 'on the job performance' (for which performance rating is an indicator). While the exact percentages can vary based on the social/economic/cultural context, typically in a group at least 75-90% of the members rate themselves as 'above average'.

This fact (that at least 75% of the people rate themselves as 'above average') creates trouble when it comes to performance ratings. These days companies are keen on 'differentiating based on performance' and this will imply that when it comes to performance ratings, the relative performance of the employees becomes a critical factor apart from the absolute performance (performance against agreed upon targets). Whether or not a fixed percentage distribution of ratings is prescribed, some sort of a 'normal curve' emerges. Typically, the positively differentiated performance ratings (that is, if we have a 1 to 5 scale with 1 being the lowest and 5 being the highest, ratings of 4 and 5) form about 25%. Thus, only about 25% of the employees will get 'above average' performance ratings. The arithmetic is simple and the conclusion is inevitable. If at least 75% of the employees consider their performance to be 'above average' and only 25% of the employees will get 'above average performance ratings', then at least 50% of the employees will be disappointed with their performance ratings. Thus, sharing of performance ratings is likely to be an unpleasant experience – both for the employee and for the manager.

Now, let us look at this from the manager's point of view. Experienced people managers know that the problem described above will happen. However, they cannot do much about it as the two critical factors (the tendency of the employees to rate their performance as 'above average' and the maximum percentage of the 'above average performance ratings' that the managers can give) are largely outside their control. Managers do what they can. This can range from 'expectation management' to 'pushing for a higher percentage of above average ratings for their team' to 'providing other rewards and recognition to compensate for the unpleasantness created by lower-than-expected performance ratings' to disowning the performance ratings (by blaming it on HR and/or senior leadership). However, these are of limited utility, as they are not addressing the core problem.

In addition, this can lead to a situation where the employees lose confidence - in the manager and in the Performance Management System. Another option for the Manager is to staff his team with people who have a low self-image (masochists are welcome!). However, if the manager wants the employees to have high self-belief and confidence when dealing with customers and low self-belief and confidence when interacting with the manager, it calls for a Janus-faced personality. While such personalities can be found in abundance in extremely hierarchical organizations, it might not be a viable strategy in 'normal' organizations!

Grappling with this problem for an extended period of time and gaining insights and wisdom from the struggle should help the Manager to be more reasonable when estimating his own relative performance (and hence the performance rating he deserves) and to be more understanding when the manager's manager tries to share and explain the manager's performance rating. But, as the studies in 'Behavioral Economics' have demonstrated, being aware of a 'bias' need not necessarily help one to overcome the bias! No wonder managers often dread the entire business of performance ratings – giving the performance ratings to their team and receiving their own performance ratings!

The research done on the 'above average effect' has thrown up some interesting findings that might help us, at least to some extent, in dealing with this problem in the context of performance ratings. It has been found that the individuals who were worst at performing the tasks were also worst at estimating their relative performance/degree of skill in those tasks. It has also been found that given training, the worst subjects improved the accuracy of their estimate of their relative performance apart from getting better at the tasks.

Another possibility here is to make the performance ratings less dependent on relative performance and more dependent on absolute performance (performance against agreed upon targets) or to increase the percentage of 'above average ratings'. However, these kinds of steps can go against the performance management philosophy of the organization (of differentiation based on performance) and hence impractical. If the context so permits, standardization of performance objectives/targets for a particular role and making the information on the performance of employees on the objectives/targets available to all can also be looked at. Research shows that self-evaluation (especially in comparative contexts) is driven primarily by an intuitive 'heuristic process' as opposed to a logical/effortful 'evidence-based process'. However, by making valid and reliable data on relative performance available and by encouraging the employees to look at it (or even to participate in an open discussion about it) before they do the self-evaluation (and evaluation of their relative performance), the influence of the 'evidence-based' part on the decision making-process can increase.

Again, we can make discussions on the challenges related to the 'above average effect' part of the performance management related communication and training for employees and the managers. Maybe, we can even build in some 'nudges' (like asking the employees to write down three things that their peers have done better than them, as part of the self-assessment) that will prompt them to deal with their cognitive bias (of superiority illusion) in a more rational manner.

Apart from this, ensuring that basics of performance management like performance planning, coaching, feedback and review are done well also helps, though they do not directly address the problem we are discussing. It is similar to 'taking antibiotics for dealing with a viral infection'. While they don't solve the core problem (virus) they do help in preventing secondary infections and hence has some utility in some cases (especially when effective anti-viral drugs are not available and the possibility of secondary infections are high)! The problem we are dealing with here is too 'human' to be completely solved by 'performance management techniques', and we have to live with it, at least to some extent, as the price for being human!

Exporting your problems

Have you ever wondered why it is not the best performers who often get the opportunity to move to other roles in the organization? Logically, it should be the best performers who should get preference in lateral moves as they have already proved their capability and also because it can accelerate their capability and career development. Sometimes, we might also see even the low-performing employees getting preference over high-performers when it comes to lateral moves. This brings us to the paradox of exporting your problems.

'Exporting the problems' is one of the most common 'crimes' in the domain of Performance Management. This refers to attempts by people managers to move the 'low-performing' and/or 'difficult to manage' members in their team to other teams in the organization. Since no people manager would want to accept a low-performer into his team, this 'crime' often involves some degree of 'deception'. This can include tactics like not giving an accurate picture of the performance of the employee (if the performance ratings are yet to be assigned) or even artificially inflating the performance rating of a poor-performing employee so that he comes into the 'good performance' category for the next one year.

An effective way to prevent this 'crime' (apart from calibrating performance ratings to ensure accuracy and getting new manager to thoroughly evaluate the employee before accepting the transfer) is to stipulate that unless the performance of an employee is good, he won't be eligible for any role changes. This will encourage the managers to focus on helping the employee to improve his performance before recommending any transfer to other teams, and, if the performance improvement efforts fail, to initiate the exit process for that employee. An exception to this rule can be made in the case of employees who were very good performers in their previous roles in the organization. In those cases, the current low-performance is likely to be a 'person-role' fit issue and they can be moved to roles similar to their previous role if possible.

An extreme form of 'exporting the problems' involves recommending an employee for a promotion with the condition that he should be moved to other teams. The rationale given by the manager could include things like the next level jobs in the current team being too complex, the concerns existing team members will have if their peer becomes their manager etc. Here also, the solution can be to specify that unless the manager is willing to move the employee into a next level role within his team (when such an opportunity comes up) the manager can not recommend a promotion for that employee.

There is another interesting (but very unfortunate) possible fallout these attempts by managers to 'export their problems'. Over a period of time, managers in the organization lose trust in the recommendations of the other managers. This makes it difficult for managers to export low-performers. Since many of the managers might not want to let go of their best performers (some sort of 'talent hugging' behavior) and since they cannot export the low performers any more, they tend to recommend the average performers in their team when new opportunities come up. This can create a situation where the best talent loses out on career opportunities and the average talent gets those opportunities. This can lead to the average talent progressing faster from career development point of view (as compared to the best talent), and this in turn can lead to the exit of the best talent from the organization. Therefore, mediocrity triumphs!

An effective performance management system that ensures accurate visibility of the performance of employees to the key stakeholders beyond the immediate manager is the first step in preventing the kind of problems mentioned above. Of course, clearly articulating the talent philosophy, building people manager capability and having the right performance measures for people managers will also be of immense help. Ideally, the talent moves should be based on detailed talent management calibration discussions (involving the other key stakeholders also, in addition to the manager) that matches the employee aspirations, strengths, performance and potential with the emerging requirements of the organization (and also provides structured feedback to the employees)!

There is another interesting aspect here. I find it a bit funny to hear people managers speaking about their willingness (or lack of it) to 'release' talent from their team. The term 'release' is more appropriate in situations like releasing someone from a prison or from a lunatic asylum. Yes, managers need to get the work done and they need good quality talent to accomplish that. So, the people management system should ensure timely availability of high-quality talent (leveraging strategic workforce planning and outcomes of talent management calibration discussions) to replace the high-performers who are moving to other teams. However, speaking about 'releasing talent' might be an indication that people managers have 'inappropriate mental models' about talent and talent mobility!

The Paradox of High-Performance Cultures

'Creating a high-performance culture' is a phrase that adorns many a corporate presentation. Once we have spoken about whatever else we wanted to say about your business strategy, adding the magic phrase 'creating a high-performance culture', seems to give it a nice 'human touch' and demonstrates our commitment to facilitating the unfolding of human potential in the organization!

So, what is the problem? Just because something looks good on PowerPoint slides, we cannot assume that it will not work in real life. The problem begins when we start asking questions. Is there really something like a 'high-performance culture'? Does it remain constant across organizations? Is it a naturally occurring phenomenon or is it something that can be created? If it can be created, what kind of creation is required? Once created, can it be sustained? It is when we try to answer these questions, we come to the paradox involved.

An issue becomes a paradox when there are multiple opinions the issue, each of which appears to be true, but they seem to be in conflict with one another. In this discussion, we will look at the various perspectives that exist regarding high-performance cultures and try to make some sense out of them. Let's start with some of the perspectives:

- High-performance culture is the ultimate source of competitive advantage and hence developing a high-performance culture should be given the highest priority.
- High-performance culture is just a fad. It sounds good. But it is very difficult to bring it down to specifics and impossible to implement. It is just something that has been invented in retrospect to explain the success of some high-performing groups.
- Culture is a characteristic of a group whereas high-performance is an outcome that depends on multiple factors. Hence, it is misleading to speak about high-performance work cultures. One should instead speak about high-performance work systems.
- There is no one culture that leads to high-performance.
- There are cultural traits leading to high-performance that hold good across organizations.
- We can define a target high-performance culture and create it in a short period of time.
- Culture is something that evolves over a period of time and deepest levels of culture consist of unconscious assumptions. It is not something that be 'copied and pasted' on a group.

To make sense out of this, we need to clarify what is 'culture' and what is 'high-performance'. While there are multiple perspectives here also, let us use the following as working definitions. A group is said to be high-performing when it consistently achieves its goals. Culture is the 'way we do things around here' – the recurring patterns of behavior in a group. If we put these two definitions together, we can define a 'high-performance culture' as those recurring patterns of behavior in a group that enables the group to consistently achieve its goals. So, the real question becomes 'is there really a set of such of behaviors that lead to high-performance of the group'?

If we want to understand the functioning of groups, we have to look at both its hardware and software. Hardware is the structure, policies, processes etc. Software is the people and the culture. Often, problems at the hardware level get conveniently misdiagnosed as software problems, because it is much easier to train people and to run culture-building sessions as compared to making significant changes in structure, policies and processes. So, if we want to have a high performing group, both the hardware and the software have to be good and also be in sync with each other.

Most of the studies in the domain of high-performance cultures list a set of characteristics and factors associated with high-performance cultures. These characteristics and factors and their relative importance vary across the different studies, Yes, sometimes they do look like wish-lists and not like proven causal factors for high-performance cultures. Nevertheless, it is instructive to take a look at them.

Some of the popular characteristics listed are passion for excellence, shared understanding and buy-in to the organization purpose, vision and goals, outward focus, decisiveness, sense of urgency, speed and agility, sense of ownership and personal accountability on the part of all the employees, discipline, diversity and inclusion, innovation and risk-taking, passion for learning and renewal etc. All these do seem reasonable. What is not proved is whether these characteristics are causally linked to high-performance or if they are just correlated with some of the high-performance situations.

Now let us look at the factors that the studies on high-performance culture list as the ones responsible for high-performance. They include high performance standards and benchmarks, alignment of goals, high person-job fit, clarity of individual performance goals coupled with real-time feedback, review and coaching mechanisms, streamlined, and simplified processes and procedures, policies that enable and not hinder performance, flatter organization structures, realigned competency frameworks and incentive schemes to reinforce appropriate behaviors, high degree of performance based differentiation in rewards, role modelling by the leaders etc. Here again all these factors seem reasonable. But they seem to be part of any good performance management system and not something unique to high-performance cultures.

Maybe, that exactly is the crux of the issue. If these factors corresponding to good performance management are coherently and consistently implemented, it will lead to high-performance. That is, when these gets consistently done and get role modelled by the leaders, it becomes 'the way things get done' and that is exactly the definition of culture that we have been using! When these are also structurally reinforced by appropriate structures, processes and policies they become sustainable. This helps us to realize the true power and importance of performance management. The performance management system, when properly designed and implemented, can be the most effective culture-building tool instead of being a collection of annoying forms and formats!

Yes, spelling out what exactly is high performance and what exactly is the target culture required in their particular context will be helpful for a group to work towards high performance. High-performance need not necessarily be relative. It is with respect to whatever goals a group sets for itself though the group might refer to external performance benchmarks before arriving at the its goals. Similarly, there is no one right blueprint for culture as the culture that will lead to high-performance for a group will depend on the group's strategy, context and stage of evolution.

The most important thing here is to go beyond broad statements of intent and empty platitudes. To make things we work, we have to identify the few most important cultural characteristics that needs to be changed and reinforced. We also need to keep in mind the interrelationships, structural reinforcements and alignments. We must ensure that the new cultural characteristics that we are trying to build is in alignment with the core values of the organization. Another important enabler is to remove impediments to high performance like 'passive resistance'. All these, when done consistently, becomes the way of life and hence fit to be called 'culture'!

So where does this leave us? Yes, groups vary in terms of performance levels and some of that variations in performance can be attributed to differences in the patterns of behavior (culture) in the group. Since these groups function in different contexts and with different goals, we can't identify a single blueprint for high-performance culture that will be valid across groups though there could be some common characteristics and factors. Yes, in any group we can examine the hardware and software of the group to see if they are optimized and aligned for the achievement of the goals that the group has set for itself. When we detect gaps in the same, steps can be taken to address the same. However, these will often require fundamental changes in the functioning of the group and that requires commitment and investment from the leaders for an extended period of time. We must remember that what often differentiates a high-performance culture is the intensity and rigor of the implementation and not content of the culture! Unless the group is fully committed to the change, in both letter and spirit, the changes can't be implemented and sustained. After all, a culture becomes real only when it is experienced!

Magical Transformation of Talent

"If there are times when you feel that you are not being valued by the organization, don't leave. Quietly do your work. You will come back into fashion!", said the experienced business leader to the new joiner during an informal conversation.

Comments like this are quite common. They also true to a large extent. Yes, there are some employees in any organization whose fortunes are relatively steady (remains the same, steadily improve, steadily worsen etc.)

But, most of the employees with long tenures have faced some degree of waxing and waning of their fortunes in the organization.

So, let's look a bit more deeply at the question "What are the factors that make the fortunes of an employee wax and wane in an organization?"

Now, 'fortunes of an employee in an organization' can mean different things (like promotions, salary increases, bonuses, being chosen for important roles/projects etc.). To simplify our discussion, let us take the 'talent classification' of the employee (placement of the employee on the 'performance-potential matrix') as the indicator of an employee's fortune in the organization, as this talent classification acts as a key driver for the decisions on promotions/increments/bonuses/roles etc. So, a drastic change in the fortunes of the employee ('magical transformation of talent') can be indicated by more than one step change in the performance and/or potential ratings (say on a 4-point rating scale) of the employee.

Let's look at some of the factors that can lead to this kind of a drastic change in employee fortunes:

Role change: If an employee is moved to a role that doesn't play to his strengths the performance can reduce significantly, especially in the short-term. One especially unfortunate case (that is more likely in the case of top talent) is to be given a 'stretch role' with an impossible degree of stretch. This, if not managed promptly, can lead not only to a drop in performance but also to loss of confidence in the employee (and to the employee losing self-confidence). There can also be a more subtle variation of 'role change' where the role (that the employee has been handling so far) itself changes - in terms of expectations from the role and the skill-set requirements - and if the employee is unable to respond well to these changes, his performance can be adversely affected.

Promotion: It is possible that the last promotion moved the employee to 'his level of incompetence'. This is especially true for the 'sublimated' employees who have not invested enough in building their skills while climbing the organization ladder.

Manager-related changes: This is essentially because of the 'manager discretion' involved in performance and potential assessments. A well-designed performance management system that also includes calibration involving the other stakeholders in addition to the manager, can help in reducing this subjectivity in manager judgement. Potential assessments are inherently more subjective and hence more prone to the variations introduced by manager changes. Also, in spite of all the systems, processes and tools that we have implemented to make people management more 'objective', the 'Chemistry' between two human beings (the manager and the employee in this case) continues to be a factor in all these decisions (and it is something that will be impacted when there is a manager change). Of course, one's 'equation' with the current manager can also change and that can add another layer of variability. Another important 'manager-driven' phenomenon is that of 'great by rotation'. This typically happens in those organizations that insist on a fixed distribution of performance and/or potential ratings and a positively differentiated rating is required for promotions. In such cases, managers might be tempted to inflate the performance/potential of different employees each year so as to make them eligible for promotions. So, employees become great by rotation! Using a well-run calibration process for talent decisions (instead of taking a purely Mathematical Approach of relying on rigid distributions and rules) can avoid these kinds of situations.

Leadership changes at CEO/CXO levels: Leaders hired with a transformation agenda might look at tenured employees as part of the problem that they need to solve, and, this can lead to a dramatic change in the way the tenured employees are looked at.

Employee-specific factors: Employees are human beings and their level of effort/involvement/engagement and hence their level of contribution to the organization can vary based on the factors in their personal life. Yes, a supportive talent management system that focuses on 'managing the whole person' can definitely help.

Larger organizational factors: Employees' fortunes depend on the fortune of the organization. While the fortune of the organization affects all the employees, the impact on employees might not be uniform. Some roles and skill-sets might become more critical. If there is a restructuring, some roles might get eliminated. This also brings us to another important aspect. These days. it is very much possible that an employee might not necessarily recover/bounce back from a phase of waning fortunes! Yes, change resilience and change agility definitely helps!

Luck! Being at the right place at the right time' has always been a key contributor to employee's fortunes. Though sometimes scenario planning and change agility can help us to be 'at the right place at the right time', it is often a matter of pure chance! Depending on one's belief system/'sense-making process', supernatural explanations are also possible. This brings to mind a famous poem in Malayalam that (while referring to the divine) says something like "It is you who makes someone rich and famous in a matter of days; and it is you who makes a king who is living in a place, a rag-picker"!

So where do these leave us? Waxing and waning of fortunes of employees (including large fluctuations in fortunes that can qualify as 'Magical Transformation of Talent') are very much possible. It can be because of organization and/or individual related factors; and sometimes, even because of plain luck. An awareness of these factors can help the employees to increase their readiness and to manage their careers better, even if many of the career moves, they make turn out to be based on emergent opportunities and risks (and not planned in advance). This is even more important these days keeping in mind the disruptive nature of the changes that many organizations are going through!

I do wonder whether 'top talent becomes successful in organizations' or 'we are just calling successful employees' top talent'! If it is the latter, then the waxing and waning of employee fortunes can definitely impact the talent classification!

Rethinking performance management

Most of our performance management practices indicate the underlying assumption that talent can be managed in the same manner as any other resource. The problem is that talent comes with problematic parts like a head and a heart (and probably, a soul) in addition to hands and legs. Also, talent, at least good talent, manages the organization as much as the organization manages the talent. It is a curious feature of human nature that we are keener to manage than to be managed. Thus, the traditional 'plan – implement – review - control' approach to management doesn't work very well when it comes to performance management.

A more appropriate approach to management will be 'understand-predict-engage-facilitate' when it comes to talent management. This requires developing deeper understanding of the human nature and human behavior in the workplace context, of the evolving employee preferences and of the enabling structures and choice architectures that can 'attract' employee behavior to desirable patterns. This will help mangers in designing initiatives like 'mass career customization' that enable talent to manage themselves facilitated by a clearly defined set of options and implications of those options.

CHAPTER 4: PARADOXES IN LEARNING AND CAPABILITY BUILDING

Once, a beginner asked a Zen master, "Master, what is the first principle?"

"If I were to tell you, it would become the second principle", replied the Zen master.

I came across this Zen story one of the books of Osho. It is about the 'first principle of Zen'. The concept is that once you know the first principle of Zen, you become enlightened. The main point of the Zen story is that wisdom cannot be taught though it can be learned. So, what about all the capability-building efforts in organisations? Of course, not everything to be learned is in the wisdom category. In business organizations, most of the capability building is at the level of knowledge and skill.

In this chapter, let us look at a few paradoxes in learning and facilitating capability building. After that, we will also look at the paradox of unlearning.

Of developmental advice and the nature of wisdom

Keeping in mind the Zen story that we started this chapter with, I decided to do an exploration of the nature of 'developmental advice' (any advice that is intended to improve the effectiveness of someone at the workplace or in life in general) and the assumptions underlying most of the developmental advice. This developmental advice can be provided by anyone like the managers, mentors, colleagues, team members, coaches, teachers, parents, elders etc.

The first thing that I realized was that we need to differentiate between two types of developmental advice - one that is more 'information oriented' and one that is more 'wisdom oriented'.

Information-oriented development advice is more like development feedback - it provides a piece of information that the person receiving the advice was not aware of. It can be internal ('pointing out a blind-spot' that the person was not aware of) or external (related to a developmental option that the person was not aware of) in nature. This kind of advice, so long as it is factually correct, is indeed helpful for a person to get started on a development journey though it might not have any influence on how much progress the person is able to make on the journey.

Wisdom-oriented development advice is deeper and more complex. Process of gaining wisdom often involves struggling with (and sometimes even unsuccessfully struggling with) the paradoxes in life.

When it comes to wisdom-oriented developmental advice, the basic assumptions are that

- The person giving the advice has gained a higher degree of wisdom (regarding the particular aspect covered in the advice) through his life experience
- This wisdom can be communicated and
- The receiver is able to 'absorb' the wisdom and is also able to act on the wisdom

To me, the problem is mainly with the last two assumptions. In general, wisdom is much more difficult to communicate as compared to information. In addition, without going through the corresponding life experience, this wisdom, even though it is 'true', might not make sense to the receiver. There is a huge difference between knowing something philosophically and arriving at the same knowledge through experience!

Probably the point of the Zen story it is this point (that wisdom can neither be 'stored' nor be 'communicated', in the normal sense of those words) is what limits the usefulness of most of the self-help books. Of course, self-helps books are often useful in providing hope (that there is light at the end of the tunnel) and encouragement. It is also said that the meaning that one derives from a great book often runs in parallel with or is even independent of what is written. Maybe, that holds true for all forms of developmental advice that we have been exploring here.

While wisdom can't be communicated, it can indeed be hinted at. While wisdom can't be given, it can be acquired. A wise teacher (or a wise coach or a wise manager) can 'create a field' or 'hold a space' that maximizes the possibility that the learner is able to derive more understanding or even wisdom from the learner's own experiences. Of course, we can't assume that the person giving the development advice is always correct or that the advice is the right one at the right for the learner. This highlights the need for the learner to be discerning when it comes to accepting and absorbing developmental advice. This is a bit tricky, as this discernment needs some kind of wisdom!

It is interesting to speculate what happens to this 'teacher-student' relationship (that is so essential for the above 'learning space' to materialize) when the teachers (or coaches) become highly-paid 'service providers' instead of being 'gurus'! Can the learners (especially when they are paying for it) hold the teachers/coaches accountable for results, and if yes, would that make the outcome (or Key Performance Indicators) move away from 'wisdom' towards 'information and skills'? Can this also lead to conflicts of interest between the teacher/coach and the learner?

While one can learn from the experiences of others, wisdom requires additional work in terms of 'personalization' before it can be absorbed and integrated. Yes, a certain degree of 'readiness' on the part of the student is required for welcoming the wisdom. If 'the teacher appears before the student is ready' the teaching (or coaching) is unlikely to work! When the learner is ready, wisdom might even appear unaided, like the proverbial butterfly that comes on its own and sits softly on one's shoulder. Now, developing this readiness is probably not just a matter of effort (and there is no algorithm for it), and, may be, some sort of 'grace' is involved in this process. Again, wisdom is more a matter of 'being wise in the moment' as compared to that of 'becoming wise for good'!

There is another category of developmental advice called 'knowledge-oriented developmental advice' that comes somewhere in between the 'information-oriented developmental advice' and the 'wisdom-oriented developmental advice. We can define information as 'processed data', knowledge as 'useful information gained through learning and experience' and wisdom as 'the discernment to apply the appropriate knowledge to a particular situation'. Even in the case of 'knowledge-oriented developmental advice', it can be said that 'knowledge is useful only in those situations where it is almost superfluous'!

The paradox of 'on-the-job learning'

Next, let's look at a convenient argument for the organization and capability building teams. The script is something like this: The organization adopts the best practices of the 70:20:10 approach to employee development which correctly assumes that less than 10% of the learning takes place through formal training and that most of the learning takes place through on-the-job- experiences (70%) and through coaching and interactions (20%). This finding can be used as an excuse for 'cutting training budgets' and for 'absolving HR managers of their responsibility in talent development' without establishing any concrete mechanism for facilitating the learning through job experiences and interactions'.

Unfortunately, learning through job experiences and interactions does not happen automatically as it requires deliberate planning, practice and facilitating in-depth reflection to derive learning from the experience. Thus, there is a need to put in place a mechanism to structure, facilitate and track this type of learning.

For example, 'the way a job is structured' is a critical factor in deriving learning through on-the-job experience. This calls for an intervention at the job design level to ensure that the jobs have sufficient responsibility, authority and scope. 'Job rotation' and 'special projects' also offer high learning potential. This will require that the organization puts in place policies that encourage job rotation and assigning people systematically to special projects. Experience maps can be designed to highlight the most important experiences to develop towards a particular role. Manager capability building is essential to enable them to help the employees to plan & execute the developmental experiences and to derive more learning from the experiences through coaching.

Accelerated learning and Rites of passage

To ensure that all of us are on the same plane of understanding, let us begin by defining the two key terms - 'learning' and 'rites of passage'. Of course, these are just 'working definitions' - for the limited purpose of our discussion here.

Learning: Learning is said to occur when there is a relatively permanent change in a person's behavior. So, we are using a 'behavioral' definition for learning, as opposed to a definition that talks merely about 'gaining knowledge'. We will focus mainly on learning at an individual level that happens through experience.

Rites of passage: A rite of passage is a 'ritual' that facilitates and marks a change in a person's status. Hence, we are using a broad definition for 'rite of passage' that includes 'facilitating the change' in addition to 'marking the change' in a person's status. Also, the word 'status' that we are using here covers not only the 'social status' but also the 'psychological status' (or state of mind or mindset).

This discussion explores two main themes - the importance/value of rituals in accelerating the learning process in organizations and usefulness of the 'rites of passage concept' in facilitating & accelerating role transitions in organizations.

Now, let us come back to our definition of learning. If learning happens through experience, then some of the ways to accelerate learning should be to

- Provide a larger amount of experience and/or
- Provide experiences with a larger learning potential and/or
- Help the person to derive more learning from the experience

Another important aspect here is to 'make the learning stick' - that is to facilitate transfer of learning/application of the learning in the workplace. I feel that 'rituals' can be very useful - for helping a person to derive meaning from experience and for making the learning stick.

Rituals can increase the mindfulness of the learner. Rituals can also increase importance/value of the learning experiences in the mind of the learner. Rituals are especially important when the learning/new behavior requires a significantly different way of functioning. Rituals can signify a break from the old way of functioning and the beginning of the new way of functioning. Therefore, in our efforts to be rational and lean, if we remove rituals from learning initiatives, we might be adversely impacting their learning potential!

Now let us come back to 'rites of passage'. A rite of passage marks and enables a leap forward in maturity. They can also indicate initiations into specialized groups. Most of the cultures in the world have rituals associated with the passage from childhood to adulthood. Growing physically into adulthood happens naturally. However, the psychological transition to adulthood does not always take place automatically along with the physical transition. The objective of the rites of passage is to enable the psychological transition. The rite of passage also serves as a clear signal/statement - to the people in transition and to the community/group they belong to - that the transition has taken place. Again, it serves as an acknowledgement from the group regarding the new status of the individual. Rites of passage are not restricted to the transition to adulthood. They are also applicable in the case of other major changes/transitions in life - like marriage, divorce, loss of a loved one and retirement.

It has been observed that many of the tribal societies use rites of passage to accelerate key transitions in life (the transition from childhood to adulthood, for example). Tribal societies that have very limited resources (and hence require everyone to contribute for the survival of the tribe) can't afford a situation where many of its members are stuck in a transition state for an extended period of time where they (the members in transition) don't contribute much to the tribe. Thus, these societies have a critical need to accelerate the life transitions. There is an obvious parallel between this situation and that in many business organizations today, where it is critical for the organizations to ensure that employees making role transitions become fully productive in their new roles as early as possible.

Thus, I feel that rites of passage are relevant in the case of transitions in organizational life including career/role transitions. As mentioned above, an excellent candidate here is the transition from an individual contributor role to a people manager role. I think that this transition is not just a matter of developing some additional skills/capabilities. It also requires a change in the state of mind/mindset - a psychological transition. I am not saying that managers are a 'higher form of evolution' (or are 'superior') as compared to individual contributors. My point is just that the manager role requires a different state of mind/mindset.

In most of the organizations we are likely to find examples of managers who have 'become managers' without having made the psychological transition to 'being a manager' - making life difficult - for themselves and the people around them - especially the people they manage. I feel that designing suitable rites of passage that are appropriate in the particular organization context & culture (in addition to the necessary skill building initiatives) can help the managers in making this psychological transition faster and more effectively and hence in bridging the gap between 'becoming' and 'being' that we have seen above.

Now that we have seen the 'business case' for using rituals to increase the effectiveness of learning initiatives and for using the 'rites of passage' framework to facilitate career and role transitions, let us look at more pragmatic issues. What kind of rituals can be used to increase the effectiveness of learning programs? How exactly should one go about designing rites of passage to facilitate role transitions? After all, we are talking about implementing these in 21st century business organizations where esoteric rituals and rituals might not be appropriate. Complete treatment of these issues will require a much longer discussion than what is possible here. So, let me provide some pointers - for the time being.

If we look closely, we are likely to find that rites and rituals are very much present in 21st century business organizations. It is just that these rites and rituals look very different from their counterparts in tribal contexts.

Let us begin by looking at some of the rituals that can increase the effectiveness of learning initiatives/accelerate the learning process. To be effective, the rituals should increase the perceived value/importance of the learning initiative, make the learners more mindful and help them to derive more learning from the experience faster. So, any ritual that meets the above requirements (and that is appropriate in the particular organization/program context) should be useful.

Hence these can include 'nominating rituals' (for example, an in-depth interaction between the employee and his manager before the program that will help the employee to better appreciate the value of the program to him and the investment the organization is making for him and to be more mindful of what can be learned from the program and how it can be applied on the job), 'opening rituals' (a senior leader doing the program launch to signify the importance that the organization is placing on the program and the participants, for example), 'experience assimilation rituals' (structuring the learning experience and reflection on the learning experience to increase mindfulness, learning and assimilation of experience), 'action planning rituals' and 'program closing rituals'. In a way, there is nothing really new/esoteric about these activities (they are part of most of the well-designed learning initiatives). The idea is just to put ceremony/rituals (back) into these activities to enhance their learning potential.

Now, let us examine how the elements of rites of passage can be used to facilitate the psychological transition associated with role changes. If we analyse the rites of passage, we will see that there are some common elements/phases (even though the rites might look very different from one another) - separation, transition and re-incorporation.

The key requirement for the first phase is to detach/separate from the current status/position in the social structure and from the current identity/self. The transition phase is the in-between state where one has separated from the previous state but hasn't yet 'reached' the desired new state. The key requirement here is to remain in this state of uncertainty (without regressing into the previous state) so that the self has an opportunity to reconfigure itself in a manner that is appropriate for the desired new state. The objective of the re-incorporation phase is to re-enter the group/society with the new status/identity. Let us examine how these elements can be built into a new manager orientation program.

Conducting the manager orientation program at a site away from the office has a lot of value. The physical separation from the previous state (previous role in the office) can help in the psychological separation also. Having the space and time where one can reconfigure the mindset (not being burdened by the demands/activities of the previous state) - in the company of people who are undergoing a similar transition - that too under expert facilitation/help - can be very useful in psychologically tuning into the new role. Performing 'difficult' tasks - tasks that can't be accomplished with the previous mindset/task that require the new mindset can also be of immense value here (as they drive home the point that the previous mindset is not effective in the new role and as they help the participant to discover the mindset that is required to be effective in the new role). The key is to create an environment in which deep learning can occur and in which shared experience contributes to the creation of a new identity.

Ceremonies to mark the successful completion of the program ('graduation rituals'), especially if they are witnessed by the senior leaders (and hence signifying their acknowledgement/recognition of the new status/state of the individual) can help in the re-incorporation of the employee to the organization in the new role. By the way, new manager orientation sessions (like rites of transition) also provide an opportunity for cultural indoctrination, where company values/leadership traits/ perspective/ 'world view' can be made very explicit ('Who we are and what do we stand for as an organization', 'How do we do things around here', 'What does it mean to be a manager in this company etc.).

It is important to get the 'positioning' of these programs exactly correct. There requirement is to help the participants separate from their previous role (and mindset) and tune into their new role (develop the new mindset) without making them feel that they are an 'elite class'/'superior to the people who are doing roles that they were doing previously'. So, while branding this program is very useful, the essential signal/message to the participants should be that "You have made a very significant and valuable transition and have become more suitable for your new role; but this does not necessarily mean that you are superior to the people you manage"!

The paradox of training the victim

'Training the victim' is one of the most common 'crimes' committed in the domain of HR/Learning and Development. Often, this 'crime' follows a standard plot. There is a steady deterioration in the performance of a unit. Customers are unhappy. There is a lot of firefighting happening. The unit head is shouting at the senior employees. But nothing seems to be working. The unit head feels that since the situation hasn't improved despite all his efforts, the employees must be incompetent and/or don't have the right attitude ('solutions mindset', for example). So, he calls the HR Business Partner demands that the employees should be trained urgently. This leads to things like attitude training, skill-based training and training the managers in the unit on people management (under fancy names like 'engaging and energizing teams'). The employees dutifully attend the training programs, though they feel that they are being blamed (or even 'punished') for no fault of theirs. Even after the training programs have been rolled out, there is no significant improvement in the performance of the unit.

These kinds of situations occur mainly because of wrong diagnosis/ wrong need identification. The main problem in these contexts might not necessarily be related to the capability level of the individual employees at all. The problem could mainly be at the strategy, structure, policy, business process or leadership level. However, it is relatively difficult/inconvenient for the organization/unit head to address the issues/make changes at these levels. So, there is a temptation to jump to the conclusion that it is an employee capability issue and to attempt a training solution. Since the real issue remains unaddressed (despite the 'training solution'), there can't much improvement in the situation.

I am not saying that there won't be issues at the individual capability level. Of course, this possibility should also be explored and if there is evidence for the existence of such a need, an appropriate learning solution could be attempted. My point is just that a proper diagnosis needs to be carried out before a solution is attempted (instead of jumping into the most convenient solution) and that when it comes to taking the responsibility for the deterioration in the performance of the unit in such situations, sometimes, the individual employees are 'more sinned against than sinned'.

Often, the way the HR function is structured in the organization increases the possibility of a wrong diagnosis. This happens mostly in those organizations where the Learning function separate from the Organization Development and HR Business Partner functions. In these contexts, when a business leader directly contacts the Learning specialist supporting the unit with a 'capability problem' (or even with the request for a particular training program), it is highly possible that the Learning specialist just carries out the request without spending much effort to check if the problem has been diagnosed correctly and if a training solution is appropriate. Sometimes, this happens because the Learning specialist does not have sufficient understanding of the entire business/people context in the unit or because the training specialist does not have the requisite diagnostic/consulting skills. In these cases, 'training need identification' becomes no more than 'order taking'. Also, if the training specialist is measured mainly on the number of training programs/number of person-days of training, then there might not be much incentive for the training specialist to 'refuse an order' or even to 'question an order'!

Hence, a close partnership between the Learning function and the Organization Development/HR Business Partner functions will help in making the diagnosis/need identification more accurate by bringing in the requisite diagnosis/consulting skills, enhanced understanding of the context and greater credibility/influence with the business leaders. This will also make the 'solution' more appropriate and enhance the effectiveness of implementation by being able to manage the change better. Of course, defining the mandate for the Learning function in a more holistic manner and using the correct performance parameters to assess/reward Learning specialists will also be required.

It is interesting to note that from a psychological point of view, 'training the victim' can be considered to be a variation (or a mild version) of the broader theme of 'blaming the victim'. This involves holding the victims responsible (at least in part) for what happened to them when something bad happens. This enables others (like the unit head in this case) to absolve themselves of any blame/responsibility and to reduce cognitive dissonance which would have resulted if they had to admit that the 'system' (strategy/structure/policy/process, in this case) that they were responsible in creating/managing might be at fault. This, in turn, helps them to avoid the need for taking the more difficult/painful remedial steps that are required to address the real issue/cause of the problem.

Sometimes, this can also lead to tragic-comic situations. A few years ago, I heard about a situation where there was a proposal to conduct 'followership training' for the entire staff in a unit. Apparently, the unit head was a very poor leader and he was making the life of his staff miserable, leading to problems in employee engagement and retention (that, in turn, were creating issues for the HR team). Since it was felt that the unit head won't be open to any sort of feedback and/or training, it was being suggested that the staff in the unit be trained in followership (as the leader won't be/can't be trained on leadership)! This might qualify as a classic case of 'trying to solve the wrong problem'!

The paradox of unlearning

"Repeated cycles of Learning, Unlearning and Relearning is a must for survival today!", thundered the sage on the stage at the HR conference. "Is it even possible to unlearn?", I wondered.

I am in complete agreement with the position that in an ever-changing environment, we constantly need to learn new things. The question in my mind was only about the necessity and feasibility of unlearning. When I persisted with this question for a while, this entire matter of unlearning seemed to get increasingly paradoxical.

So, what is paradoxical about unlearning? As we have seen earlier, a paradox occurs when there are multiple perspectives/opinions that exist alongside - each of which is true - but they appear to contradict/to be in conflict with one another. Now, let us look at some of the opinions about unlearning

- Unlearning is as natural as learning.

- Unlearning is simply impossible. You can't really remove something from your mind unless there is some sort of brain damage or extreme forms of mind control (like 'brainwashing')!

- New knowledge replaces old knowledge as individuals learn more; much like overwriting. It is not considered to be the same as forgetting, where information is lost regardless of its usefulness.

- Change in a particular behavior does not in fact remove the learning altogether; it simply reduces the likelihood of the behavior in certain contexts. Hence, the proposal that new learning 'overwrites' old learning is problematic.

- Existing knowledge or behaviors interfere with learning and, therefore, unlearning needs to happen before new learning can occur.

- Unlearning and learning occur simultaneously.

- The distinction between learning, unlearning and relearning is arbitrary.

- Unlearning itself is very valuable. It allows us to see things as they really are. The essence of unlearning is about 'emptying' and not about 'emptying so that we can fill it up'.

- Unlearning should not be viewed as an end in itself. It is just an intermediate step in learning.

- Unlearning is not about forgetting. It's about the ability to choose an alternative mental model or paradigm. When we unlearn, we step outside the current mental model in order to choose a different one.

- We are usually unconscious of our mental models and that makes unlearning difficult. Also, we tend to view the new model through the lens of the old and that makes switching models even more difficult.

- We don't have to worry about unlearning. Moving towards the new learning would automatically take us away from the old learning (and hence unlearning would happen automatically). Individuals learn new ways of choosing a response to a particular situation, rather than unlearning a particular response.

So, how do we resolve this?

Even though there is quite a bit of discussion about unlearning these days, there are few theories confirmed by empirical evidence to identify how individuals unlearn and what factors may influence this unlearning. Therefore, we have to look at other options. One such option is to look at the underlying definition of 'learning' when we talk about unlearning.

If we define learning as 'acquiring knowledge', then unlearning is not possible (in the sense that it can't be forgotten) and also not even necessary (unless the existing knowledge was wrong or misleading, in which case it can be modified keeping in mind the new knowledge). When new knowledge is acquired, the old knowledge is not erased, but maintained ('in parentheses') for situations where it is believed that the new knowledge does not apply.

If we look at learning as essentially a 'sense-making process' (where individuals interpret and create meaning of their experiences) and not as a 'fact-gathering process', unlearning is about modifying the way we 'make sense'.

If we define learning as 'sustainable change in behavior', then new behavior can just replace old behavior. The only case where unlearning is required would be that of conditioned responses that interfere with learning new behaviors. Some of these conditioned responses have roots in the underlying (unconscious) mental models. We are often operating with mental models that have grown outdated or obsolete. It takes unlearning to see the model as only one if possibilities and not as the only possibility. So unlearning is not mainly about replacing one mental model with another; it is about having the ability to consciously chose from a range of mental models based on which is more appropriate in a given situation.

Unlearning is a process as opposed to a discrete event. The process of unlearning is about liberation from the conditioning. It involves intentional evaluation of self, task and the environment to determine if a change in the current behavior is necessary and possible. Mindfulness, ability to read contextual cues, openness to explore other possibilities and meta-cognitive ability are key enablers for this unlearning process.

It is also interesting to look at why there is so much interest in unlearning. It is probably because of the assumption that new learning can't happen unless unlearning happens. As we saw earlier, this is not necessarily the case – except in the case of conditioned responses that create rigidity and impact 'learnability'. Another key reason for the interest in unlearning is the belief that unlearning is essential for promoting innovation and for enabling organizations to respond more effectively to unanticipated change or crisis events (by to recognizing and modifying previous habits, approaches and behaviors that are no longer optimal).

Unlearning can happen at both the individual (assumptions, mental models, habits, response patterns etc.) and at the organization level (beliefs, paradigms, norms, rules, procedures, strategies etc.). While the unlearning at individual and organization levels can reinforce each other, they can also happen independently. For example, organizational unlearning can occur in the absence of individual unlearning through the removal of key influencers. Yes, it is important to look at the interface between individual and organizational learning in order to better understand and manage the interactions.

In a way, constant unlearning and relearning is a wasteful process. It is more efficient to modify or re-purpose old learning where possible (like a software 'update' as opposed to 'uninstall and reinstall'). Hence, relearning is better described as refocused learning (as opposed to replacing old learning with new learning). Individuals learn new ways of choosing a response to a particular situation, rather than unlearning a particular response. The focus is on modifying the response to be more effective and not on replacing one response with another (which might not necessarily lead to better outcomes). Hence, relearning is not antithetical to learning (it can happen without unlearning) and it is in fact more like learning that is made more appropriate to the current context!

All adult learning involves relating new information with existing information and thereby modifying the existing understanding. Hence, there is no requirement for a 'clean slate' or 'empty vessel' (unlearning!) to enable new learning. Even in case of children, it seems a bit weird to suggest that a child has to unlearn 'crawling' before the child can learn 'walking'!

If we stick with the behavioral definition of 'learning' (as 'sustainable change in behavior'), adopting a new pattern of behavior is just 'learning' and hence we can even argue that the concepts of unlearning and relearning are not really required (except in the cases of brainwashing and cognitive impairment, respectively) and that they might be even misleading! Of course, we can examine and work on any possible impediments and enablers to learning in a particular context.

CHAPTER 5: PARADOXES IN CAREERS AND CAREER PLANNING

Every employee rises to the level of his own incompetence.

-The Peter Principle

Can one plan one's career? Should organizations plan the careers of its employees? In a highly dynamic and uncertain business environment, does it make sense to do career planning? How should the organization balance the interests of the employee and that of the manager and the organization while deciding on employee movements? These are some of the tricky questions that govern the domain of career planning. Many of these do throw up paradoxes.

Let's look at some of these paradoxes in more detail. We will start with the fundamental issue of whether it makes sense to attempt career planning in today's environment. Then we will look the implications of skipping responsibility levels as one progresses in one's career. This will be followed by a discussion on a very popular, though somewhat 'informal' concept in the domain of career development – that of career-limiting moves! Finally, we will look at the complementary dimension of succession planning, which is very critical from the point of view of the organization.

Career planning and the myth of Sisyphus

Career planning is one of the most interesting rituals in organizations. But before we come to career planning, let us look at the myth of Sisyphus. We come across Sisyphus in Greek mythology. The myth says that because of his trickery Sisyphus was cursed by the gods. As a result of that he had to repeat a maddening procedure forever. He was compelled to roll a huge rock up a steep hill, but before he reached the top of the hill, the rock always escaped him and he had to begin again.

Actually, similar stories exist in other cultures also. For example, in my home state (Kerala) there is a similar story about Naranathu Bhranthan. Naranathu Bhranthan was considered to be a 'siddha' (an 'enlightened' or 'realized' being) though some of his behaviors appeared to be rather 'strange'. He used to follow the same procedure as that of Sisyphus (though not on a full-time basis!). But he was doing it out of choice. Also, in his case the stones would not automatically roll back. So, he would manage to get many big stones to the top of the hill. Then he would push them down one by one and he would laugh loudly as they roll down the slope. We will come back to Naranathu Bhranthan later. Myths are important as they contain eternal truths, though myths might be too true to be real.

Now let us come back to career planning. Organizations invest a lot of time an effort in career planning. There are very good reasons for doing so. A large number of studies have shown that 'opportunity for career development' is one of the most important things that employees look for in an organization. So, the organizations have to do something about this. The typical response is to map out career paths. Since organizations are keen on approaching this 'strategically'/with a long-term perspective, these career paths provide the 'growth paths' extending over many years. Since there are many types of employee profiles, employee preferences, positions and career options, often these lead to a huge amount of detail. This of course implies a large amount of time/resource investment.

But there is a paradox here. In many industries the attrition rates are very high. So, in many organizations most of the employees will leave before they complete 3 years in the organization. Hence these long-term career plans get wasted in the case of most of the employees. This is where Sisyphus comes in. We put in a lot of effort in formulating detailed career paths (like Sisyphus rolling the huge rock up the hill). But before they could make significant progress along these nice career paths most of the employees leave (or 'escape' like the rock in the case of Sisyphus). So, does 'career planning' amount to some sort of a 'Sisyphus-like curse' for HR professionals?

Maybe, the situation will improve if we can target career planning efforts to those employees who are likely to stay on with the organization for a long time. While it can be argued that career planning itself would reduce attrition, this does not seem to work very well in many organizations. May be career planning (at least in the traditional form) will have a significant influence only on some employees (who already have some sort of a long-term perspective and also have a good degree of person-organization fit!). Of course, there are more innovative approaches to career development that are being experimented.

Another way to look at this situation is to say that the 'career planning ritual' is both 'necessary and beneficial', though the manifestation of the results might not essentially be in terms of employees moving along the prescribed career paths. The ritual itself might help in building positive energy and it might also be considered a necessary condition (though often not a sufficient condition) for positive organizational outcomes. Maybe we are more like Naranathu Bhranthan than like Sisyphus. This would imply that we are formulating these career paths knowing that most of the employees won't really follow them. So, we are like Naranathu Bhranthan who was following the 'Sisyphus-like' procedure out of choice. By the way, the word 'bhranthan' in Malayalam language means a 'madman'. So, we can see that though Naranathu Bhranthan appeared to be 'mad' to many people (and hence he was called a 'bhranthan'), he was the 'master of his madness' and that he was laughing at life itself (remember - he was also considered to be a 'siddha').

Perhaps career planning in rapidly changing high attrition environments would always be a maddening activity. But each one of us can attempt to be a 'master of the madness' rather than being a slave. Maybe, we can also laugh like Naranathu Bhranthan used to do (though not so loudly - lest we might be considered to be 'mad' by the 'masters' in our organizations!) when the employees grow beyond (or even 'jump' out of) the elaborate career paths that we had created with so much effort!

Career development and 'sublimation'

Since the words 'career' and 'sublimation' have many meanings/interpretations, let us begin by defining these terms - for the (limited) purpose of our discussion.

Career- pursuit of consecutive progressive achievement where one takes up positions of increasing responsibility, complexity & contribution

Sublimation- change directly from the solid to the gaseous state without becoming liquid (so we are using the 'Chemistry' meaning of 'sublimation' - as opposed that in 'Psychology')

Now that we have got the definitions out of the way, let us come back to the issue at hand. These days, it is quite common for people to skip some of the steps in (what used to be) the 'typical career path'. That is, they jump from a particular position to another position that is more than one step away/higher. So, they transition directly ('sublimate') to a significantly 'higher' position without going through (what were considered to be necessary) intermediate positions.

These kind of career moves make a lot of sense in today's scenario - where many organizations are in state of flux - making traditional 'career paths' and 'career ladders' less relevant. Again, organizations are more open to this kind of career moves these days, especially where this results in cost saving and lower time to fill a vacancy. Of course, it makes eminent sense also from the individual's point of view - in terms of faster career growth.

So, if this 'sublimation' seems to make sense - from the points of view of both the individual and the organization - what is the issue? I think that this 'sublimation' can create problems - for the individual and for the organization.

For the individual, skipping intermediate positions in the career path can result in loss of learning opportunities - and some of these 'missed learnings' can prove costly - in terms of the adverse impact on long term career success and on personal effectiveness at work. Some of the intermediate positions might be key from a 'career & professional maturity' and perspective building (and wisdom development!) points of view. While the 'higher' positions will also provide valuable learning opportunities (may be even learning opportunities at a broader/'higher' level), they cannot always substitute for the learnings provided by the intermediate positions. I would even speculate that time spent in the intermediate roles might have a positive impact on the 'ability to learn' - including the ability to learn from opportunities at a broader/'higher' level. The situation is not dissimilar to that of children who are 'forced' (by life situations) to grow up too fast. They manage to act like grownups, but often they have hidden flaws in their (psychological) development.

Often, after one has taken up a 'higher role' (in terms of organization hierarchy) it becomes difficult* (see the note below) to take up these intermediate roles - unless one moves to another ('bigger'/'more reputed') organization. So, it is possible that these necessary learning opportunities are lost forever for the particular individual.

This brings us to the problem of 'unknown unknowns', a key side effect of 'sublimation', that can create problems for both the individual and for the organization. Usually, 'unknown unknowns' are more dangerous than 'known unknowns'. Based on our discussion above, it can be seen that the 'sublimated individuals' can create serious risks for the organization. While the 'sublimated individuals' are usually very confident, their confidence often stem from 'simplicity on this side of complexity' as opposed to 'simplicity on the other side of complexity'. These 'unknown unknowns' can seriously undermine the quality of decision making. This becomes a major cause for concern when these individuals are in positions where their decisions can have high organizational impact. From the individual's point of view, a key risk is that of self-destructing their fast-track careers! Other risks for the individuals include becoming too big for most of the roles available in their domain too early in their careers (limiting their options for changing jobs) and of course that of 'reaching their level of incompetence' too fast/too early in their careers!!

Therefore, there can be problems/costs involved with 'sublimation'. But there are also potential benefits. In addition to this, we should keep in mind that there are approaches like job rotations, stretch assignments and action learning projects that can provide accelerated career development while avoiding some of the problems associated with 'sublimation' - at least to a large extent. Hence it comes down to a cost benefit analysis - which can be highly context specific - both for the particular individual and for the particular organization - making a standard solution/recommendation difficult. But the awareness of the options and the possible problems/benefits can facilitate better cost benefit analysis and more informed decision making.

Influence of 'early career experiences'

What has been the impact of your 'early-career experiences' on you? For the purpose of this discussion, let us define 'early-career experiences' as 'experiences during the 'most impressionable part' of one's career and this would imply (for many people) experiences during the first few years of one's career/the experiences during one's first job. So please take a couple of minutes to think about your 'early-career experiences'. What do you remember about them? Do you think that they have impacted you in any significant manner? If yes, what has been the nature of the impact?

The importance of early life experiences on the psychological/behavioral development of a person is well known. But considering that one is usually much older when one starts working, can a similar phenomenon occur - in the domain of one's basic assumptions about organizational life/work/career?

While I have been thinking about this issue for quite some time, the 'trigger' for this came recently in the form of a discussion in an e-group that I am part of. This e-group consists mainly of my ex-colleagues from an organization in which I had worked a long time ago. We were discussing issues like "the reasons for the existence of strong bonds among us even though most of us had left the organization a long time ago"; "why do we often talk about the 'great experience' that we have had in that organization" etc. Now, there were multiple factors (at multiple) levels involved in the situation. I felt that one of the key factors involved (apart from the factors related to the organization context, nature of work, nature of inter-dependencies in the group etc.) was the profile of the members of the group/organization at that stage - most of us were at an 'impressionable stage' in our careers!

It was the first job for many of us and I felt that it 'shaped' our definitions of 'what is good' in an organization/workplace context (that is, the tacit/subconscious definitions of 'good' boss, 'good' team member, 'good' team, 'good' employer, 'good' learning opportunities and even that of 'good' work). Since other organizations (that we joined later in our career) are unlikely to provide environments that exactly match these definitions, the work experiences in them are likely to be perceived as falling short of 'the good old days'.

Therefore, my hypothesis is that early career experiences can have a significant impact on our careers by influencing our basic workplace preferences and attitudes. Of course, there are other factors (like personality related factors) that can also influence our workplace preferences and attitudes. It will also be interesting to examine if the impact/influence of early career experiences reduces as one progresses in one's career (and gains more experiences/data points).

Career-Limiting Moves

The most popular informal concept in the domain of people management seems to be that of a 'career-limiting move'(CLM). A Career-Limiting Move is an act that is likely to adversely impact the career prospects of a person. This 'act' can be that of 'omission' or 'commission', though the latter is more common. Also, this 'act' might be done by the individual (whose career is getting impacted) or by others who have power over the individual (by his manager or the organization, for example). The 'richness' of the concept comes from the various ways in which this term is used and also from the causes/motivations that lead to CLMs.

Let's look at some of the ways in which the term CLM is used:
- The most common use of the term CLM is as a warning to someone. We tell someone that a particular action will be a CLM for

- him/her, to warn the person against following a particular course of action.
- Another use of the term CLM is as a prediction. When we hear about someone moving to a particular role, we might say that it will be a CLM for him, implying that this move is going to adversely impact his career.
- Similarly, CLM can be realization on hindsight. When we look back, we might realize that a particular action in the past turned out to be a CLM.
- Yet another use of the term is CLM is to describe a particular aspect of the culture of an organization. We might say that questioning senior leaders is a CLM in a particular organization.

Now let's look at some of the key factors that lead to CLMs:

Alignment issues: Lack of alignment between the individual and the organization (as represented by the managers/leaders) on 'what good looks like'. Similarly, a clash between individual and organization values can also lead to CLMs.

Designed to fail roles: The organization failing to differentiate between a 'stretch role' and a 'designed to fail' role, moving a person to such a 'designed to fail' role, and, that move becoming a CLM for him/her.

'Self-Destructive Intelligence Syndrome' (SDIS): This is 'what makes smart people do stupid things' that turn out be career-limiting. While sometimes this could just be a matter of misjudging the situation, sometimes this could also be a deliberate act of violating the rules/regulations.

Plain bad luck: Just being 'at the wrong place/at the wrong time' can turn out to be career-limiting! Also, unpredictable elements in the context can turn what could otherwise have been a perfectly good move into a career-limiting one.

So, is there a 'bright side' to CLMs? Yes, what appears to be a CLM might not necessarily turn out to be like that. Even when there is some adverse impact because of the CLM, it might often be a temporary setback. It is even possible that what appeared to be a CLM turns out to be something that enhances one's career. This happens mainly because CLMs often involve pushing the unstated boundaries' and sometimes it can work out very well. Also, standing up for what one believes is right is something that is too important to be let go because of CLM warnings. We must also remember that not all CLMs have a bad ending! Yes, having great managers/leaders very much enhances this possibility!

I have also come across situations where the CLM warning was based on the fears (ghosts!) in the mind of the person giving the warning and not based on reality. Similarly, sometimes a CLM warning could be an attempt to protect the interests of the person who is giving the warning. So, we must do a reality check before acting on CLM warnings we get!

To name, or not to name, that is the question: The paradox of succession planning

"Do you think that I should have announced my successor?", asked the Senior leader.

This was a very interesting question in the context we were in, and it prompted me to think deeply about the underlying issues. In this particular case, the situation was something like this: This gentleman had created a structure in which many of his direct reports were at the same level – handling roles of similar size. This ensured that all of them could hope for moving into his role and hence contributed to their engagement and retention. However, this also ensured that when this gentleman moved on to another role, none of his direct reports were ready to take over from him & hence his role had to be filled with an external candidate. With their illusions broken (and considering the fact that the situation could repeat a few years later), many of the direct reports started looking for jobs outside the company.

Now, there are multiple levels of issues here. The most basic one is the need for succession planning. There should not be too much controversy here, as most of us are likely to agree that succession planning (especially for critical roles) is a worthwhile endeavour. The second one is the need for a structured approach to develop people who are in the succession plan so that they become ready for the role within a specified time-frame. Here also there should not be much disagreement when it comes to the validity of the need, though the implementation is easier said than done, as it involves quite a bit of investment/focus to ensure that the requisite capability building takes place within the timelines.

Things get more complicated when we think about whether or not to tell the people who are in the succession plan that they are part of the succession plan. The problem here is that doing this can create high expectations (and even some sort of 'entitlement mentality') among the people in the succession plan and also create disengagement (or even attrition) among people who are not in the succession plan. The latter becomes a significant problem if they are very valuable contributors in their current roles, though they did not make it to the succession plan for the next level role. However, not informing those in the succession plan might defeat the very purpose of succession planning.

The purpose of including an employee in the succession plan for a position is to enable him to develop readiness for the position within an accelerated time-frame. It will work much better if the employee is aware of the purpose for which the development is being undertaken. It definitely helps to tell an employee that he is part of a succession plan, so long as the communication is done in the right manner. This will also avoid the risk of developing an employee towards a position that he is not interested in. Again, this will prevent the unfortunate scenario in which such an employee leaves the organization because he thought that he was not being developed for the next level role!

However, the communication has to be done in the right manner. The communication should mention that the company sees the potential in him to develop towards the particular position and that the company will provide accelerated learning opportunities to enable him to develop readiness for the same. It has to be made clear that no promise is being made that the employee will be moved to the target position within a specified period of time. It should also be mentioned that there could be multiple people in the succession plan for the position and that the actual move to the position will depend on business requirement, vacancy and his relative readiness as compared to other possible candidates for the position. Stretch and discomfort are inherent in accelerated development. If an employee is aware of and is committed to the purpose behind the development, he will be able in a better position to derive meaning from the stretch experience, to learn faster and even to enjoy the ride!

Let us come back to the question asked by the business leader. There are no easy answers to his question. However, let me hazard a guess based on our discussion so far. It would have been better if he had done the succession planning for his role and told the people in the succession plan that they were being developed for his role. Of course, this would require that the identification of people for the succession plan was done in manner that was rigorous and fair (and also seen to fair!). For example, all his direct reports (at least those who were interested in developing towards his role) could have been put through a well-designed Assessment Centre.

Now, let's look at the matter of deciding the ideal number of people in the succession plan for a particular position. Announcing only one successor would have been a very risky option. It would have made the organization dependent on only one person and/or it could have made the person in the succession plan a bit complacent. Putting too many people in the succession plan also would have been sub-optimal. It would have made the investment required for developing all these people too high and also reduced the chance for any particular individual to succeed in moving to the target role. Hence the best option would have been to identify a few (say, 2-3) people who were relatively more ready at that point (say, based on the Assessment Centre results) to be on the succession plan and to tell them they were being developed for his role. This would also allow the others direct reports to either make peace with this situation (as a fair process has been followed to identify the people in the succession plan) or to exit the organization gracefully - at a time of their choice (without any hurry and possibly with a very good offer). Yes, this is not a perfect solution. But it seems to be the best solution available!

CHAPTER 6: PARADOXES IN REWARDS & RECOGNITION

It is difficult to get a man to understand something when his salary depends upon his not understanding it.

-Upton Sinclair

In this chapter, we come to the very important matter of money. Yes, not all the employees are equally motivated by money. However, there is more than what meets the eye when it comes to the monetary aspects of organizational life. For example, money often acts as a proxy for the relative value of an employee in the organization, and hence in addition to meeting existence level needs, money might also be satisfying esteem level needs! Also, money is where most of the heartburn in organizations start. Of course, this domain is also rich in paradoxes from both the employee and the organization points of view.

Just to get a better flavour of this domain, let us take a quick look at some of the interesting questions related to this domain. Should the organization use money as a differentiator by paying in the top quartile of the market? Or should they just pay at the median and use the other factors to differentiate? Is pay purely a matter of supply and demand of talent or is there a compensation philosophy that looks at other factors also? What impact can non-monetary recognition make? Can it be a substitute for rewards? To what extent the company should differentiate the rewards based on performance? How should the company look at rewards? Mainly as a 'cost to be managed' or as an 'important tool for driving employee behavior'?

In this chapter, we will explore some of the paradoxes related to rewards in detail. We will start by looking at a more fundamental issue underlying this domain that is indeed paradoxical. Why the 'carrot and stick' method, which is the most basic form of reward and punishment, works so well in influencing employee actions. After that, we will look at two differing perspectives on optimising salary related decisions over the course of one's entire career. Then we will move to the very important aspect of conducting salary negotiations during the various phases of employment. Keeping in mind the principle of integrative thinking which is an essential component of the paradoxical perspective, we will situate these salary negotiations in the context of their impact on the formation and modification of the psychological contract between the employee and the employer. Next, we will look at the paradoxical concept of 'Total Rewards' that significantly extend the scope of rewards. Finally, we will explore the paradoxical aspect of differentiation.

The paradox of the power of 'carrot and stick'

Quite a bit of the paradoxical nature of people management in organizations comes from something deeper, the paradoxical issue of can people be motivated or inspired the way the organizations wants. This brings us to the strange power of carrot and stick.

The objective here not to recommend or to praise the 'carrot and stick method'. It is just to examine the actual situation in this domain (in terms of both theory and practice) and to explore the possible reasons for the 'power of carrot and stick'. We will also look at possible responses to this situation - from both the employee's and the employer's points of view.

While today's organizations are unlikely to talk about the 'carrot and stick method', if we analyse the methods that are actually being used by organizations to 'motivate' their employees, we are likely to find a high amount of 'carrot and stick' element in them. Of course, the 'carrots' and 'sticks' have become more sophisticated. But, in time of 'organization stress' some of this sophistication often disappears and more crude forms of 'carrot and stick' (that were thought to have become extinct) reappear!

Now, let us examine why the 'carrot and stick method' works so well. I think that the power of 'carrot and stick' emanates mainly from the fact that it takes advantage of two of the most basic human emotions, desire and fear. To be more explicit, 'carrot' scores a direct hit on 'desire' and 'stick' does the same on 'fear'. It can be argued that if we use the terms 'desire' and 'fear' in a broad sense, most of the human emotions (and hence most of the human behavior and motivation!) can be 'modelled' in terms of these two (and the human responses to them).

If we push the above argument a little further, it can be deduced that the so called 'content theories' of motivation (especially those that talk about fulfilment of 'needs', like the Maslow's hierarchy of needs, ERG theory, McClelland's theory of needs etc.) can't distance themselves too much from 'desire' element (and hence from 'carrot and stick'). Similarly, if we take a close look at some of the 'process theories' of motivation (like the expectancy theory) we might be able to detect elements of 'carrot and stick' in them also (especially in the 'valance' part of the 'expectancy - instrumentality - valance' chain/of the cognitive process that leads to motivation, as per the Expectancy theory).

If we consider motivation as a 'state of mind' (that is, as something that happens in the mind of a person), 'carrot and stick' (or anything external to that person, like what the manager/ employer does) can't directly cause motivation to occur - it can only create a situation where motivation is likely to be 'triggered'. Again, the method for applying carrots and/or sticks for maximum effectiveness (especially if we take the sustainability of the effectiveness account), can become quite complex. There have been quite a few studies on the effectiveness of various types of positive and/or negative reinforcement strategies to elicit desired responses. So, the 'power' of 'carrot and stick' does not imply that the application (of 'carrot and stick') is always easy!

Now, let us look at this situation from the other side – from the point of view of the employee who is at the 'receiving end' of these motivation strategies. From the above discussion, it can be seen that if an employee wants to be immune from the power of 'carrot and stick', he/she should develop immunity from 'desire and fear' – at least those types of desires and fears that can be leveraged/manipulated by the employer. Easier said than done – I must admit - for most of the 'real' people in 'real' organizations!

the way, in the novel 'Siddhartha' by Hermann Hesse, there is a beautiful description of how this method of motivation (implemented through an incentive scheme - with a significant upside and downside for the employee) attempted by an employer (Kamaswami, the rich merchant) fails to have any impact on an employee (Siddhartha) who had transcended 'desire and fear' ("Siddhartha can think, Siddhartha can wait, Siddhartha can fast"). It is also interesting to note that this novel was first published in 1922 - much before 'management' in the current sense of the term became popular.

My point is not that most of the human beings are nothing more than bundles of 'desires and fears'. We are capable of other emotions (like love, sense of pride, sense of duty, quest for purpose/meaning etc.) that might go beyond 'fear and desire'. Therefore, it should be possible to find ways of motivation based on these 'higher' emotions. However, these higher emotions might not be very easy to 'manipulate' in an organization setting.

Most of the organizations have an essentially top-down goal-setting and goal cascade process. While individuals might have some degree of freedom to shape their roles/deliverables, individual goals must add up to the corporate goals. Also, organizations usually hire people to do a particular job (which might even have a formal job description that details the job responsibilities). These factors can lead to a situation where a large part of what needs to be done by a particular employee has been 'fixed', 'mandated' or even 'imposed'. If what you need to do is fixed, then whether the leader 'inspires you' or 'motivates you' to get the same thing done can become essentially a matter of semantics!

I also feel that 'inspiring someone' (creating a situation where someone might become inspired- to be precise) is a more unpredictable process (in terms of outcomes) as compared to 'motivating someone' (to do a particular task – say through carefully applied positive and/or negative reinforcement - including the promise/threat of applying/withdrawing positive and negative reinforcement or 'carrots and sticks'!). No, I am not endorsing the 'morality' of these 'motivation' techniques. I am just saying that they are possible. I must also mention that there could be situations where these techniques might fail. For example, it is easy to create 'incentives' (financial and non-financial) for someone to write a book. But whether this can result in a 'great book' (if the author is not really inspired to write the book) is debatable. However, the fact remains that 'inspiration' is often a complex (and elusive!) phenomenon.

While, your manager can 'inspire' you, what you will end up doing based on (triggered by) that inspiration couldn't always be predicted accurately. Therefore, if the objective is to get you to do a particular task, I am not sure if the pure inspiration route will always work. Any attempt to make the inspiration more controlled, will bring in the element of manipulation that this inspiration approach is trying to avoid. Of course, if we are talking about a community with no predefined goals (as opposed to organizations that usually have predefined/ mandated goals) then this inspiration approach might work – though no one can predict what will exactly will the outcome be (at the individual and at the community level – considering 'interaction effects' and 'emergence')!!

It might be possible to make a distinction between actions that we take because of some sort of compulsion and those we take because we really want to do so (between compliance and commitment for example). The problem here is that compulsion does not necessarily mean coercion (at least not in the usual meaning of the term 'coercion') - any sort of 'inducement' can also imply compulsion. In a way, all we can observe is the action and the reason behind the action is something that we infer - especially in the case of other people. Even if we are talking about our own actions and the reasons for those actions there is the problem of rationalization, (for example, we can attribute the 'good' actions to intrinsic motivation and the 'not so good' actions to external compulsions). Hence, the distinction between the two types of actions can get blurred.

Studies in Behavioral Economics have shown that 'relational rewards' work better than 'monetary rewards' in many circumstances, though relational rewards have the disadvantage of raising relational expectations. Please note that this does not negate the 'power of carrot and stick'. We can always say that while relational rewards ('relational carrots') and different from 'monetary/transactional rewards' ('transactional carrots') - they are still 'carrots' - carrots that appeal to higher order needs (say in Maslow's hierarchy of needs).

Again, it has been suggested that monetary incentives work best in the case of simple tasks (tasks involving straightforward physical or mental activity; that is, tasks that do not require creativity) where higher performance is just a matter of trying harder and where the performance can be measured accurately. This also need not necessarily create problems for the 'power of carrot and stick theory' as this is more about the relative effectiveness of carrots.

We must also keep in mind that there is an intense debate going in between 'rational choice economists' and 'behavioral economists' - regarding the applicability of the findings from behavioral economics experiments. It has been argued that we are quite rational in most circumstances (that is, in our natural habitat/ in familiar situations) and these predictable irrationalities surface mainly in in unfamiliar circumstances and that the conditions created in some of the behavioral economics experiments are quite unnatural (that is, not representative of the conditions faced by most people most of time in the real world). Even the very definition of rationality is open to debate! Rationality can be defined narrowly, as a consistent system of preferences or as a consistent response to incentives, even if these preferences might not be 'good' for the decision maker as judged by the society!

Shape of the salary graph or area under the salary curve?

One of the key considerations that affect job change decisions is that of salary. However, what exactly is one trying optimise when it comes to salary progression over one's career is no simple. Actually, there is a polarity here! It is related to one's outlook towards salary growth, seen in the context of one's entire career.

The two extremes (polarities) here are 'shape approach' and 'area under the curve approach'. It is essentially a matter of what one is trying to optimise - 'shape of the graph' or 'area under the graph'. To better understand this, let us visualize a diagram ('salary graph') with salary on the y-axis and time on the x- axis.

Those who take a 'shape of the graph' approach/philosophy want to ensure that their salary goes up each time they make a job change (either within an organization or across organizations). Therefore, they want the salary graph to have a nice shape - with a positive 'slope' at all times. These kinds of people will not want to take up a very high paying job if they feel that the salary growth is not sustainable and that they might have to take a pay cut later when they move from the very high paying job.

If we go back to our salary diagram (with salary on the y-axis and time on the x- axis), the area under the graph signifies the total earnings over a period of time/over the span of the career. It is apparent that what the people who take an 'area under the graph' approach/philosophy are trying to maximise is their total earnings/salary. These kinds of people will take up a very high paying job even if they feel that the salary growth is not sustainable - so long as their total earnings (over the span of their career) are likely to be higher.

Of course, the above approaches ('shape of the graph' and 'area under the graph') apply not only in the case of salary but also in the case of other dimensions of career growth like 'size of the role', 'position of the role in the organization hierarchy' and 'learning experiences provided by the role'. It is interesting to note that 'shape of the graph' approach/philosophy is reflected in many of the typical definitions of the term 'career', as it talks about ' pursuit of consecutive progressive achievement' and about 'taking up positions of increasing responsibility'). But we have seen that this not the only approach possible or even the most effective one in today's environment. So, if one takes the 'area under the graph' approach (which is more attuned to today's scenario), it can provide one more flexibility in decisions related to job change!

Salary negotiations and the psychological contract

"I feel cheated. If I had known this, I would not have joined this company", said the frustrated employee. "We had given you a good hike over your previous salary. We had also explained the details of your compensation and benefits when we gave you the offer letter. Once you have signed the employment contract, it is not appropriate on your part to raise issues about it so soon. What somebody else get paid is none of your business", replied the HR Manager.

This is a scene that gets enacted quite frequently across organizations, with unpleasant consequences for both the employer and the employee. I have often wondered what can be done about it. Based on my experience in the domain (from both sides of the fence!), I think that an exploration of the terrain from multiple perspectives is required to find a reasonable solution to this puzzle. I also feel that while the 'best solution' is likely to be context specific, some general guidelines can be formulated.

Let us begin by taking a closer look at the concept of 'psychological contract'. We will also conceptualize salary negotiations in terms of the key stages in the 'employee life cycle' in which salary negotiations take place.

The psychological contract is a set of mutual expectations held by the employer and employee that might not be captured in the formal employment contract. While the psychological contract is 'not on paper', it is very much real and significant as it impacts how the employer-employee relationship evolves. It also influences the key decisions made by the employees like the decision on whether or not to put in discretionary effort and whether or not to leave the organization. Hence maintaining the psychological contract is critical for enabling positive employee relations. Please note that in the case of reasonably well-managed organizations (where a breach of the legal employment contract is unlikely to happen), employee exits almost always happen because of the perceived violations in the psychological contract.

Salary negotiation is not the only factor that influences the formation and evolution of the psychological contract. Psychological contract might have other dimensions like organization climate and culture, degree of empowerment, career growth, learning opportunities etc. However, salary negotiation is a very significant factor in terms of the degree of impact on the psychological contract.

For our exploration here, we will use a broad definition of the term 'salary' – to include not only the cash part of the compensation but also the benefits and perquisites. Hence our focus will be on those parts of the psychological contract that have something to do with expectations the employees have regarding the salary (including variable salary), benefits & perquisites and the expectations that the employer has on what the employees need to do to earn the same. They also include mutual expectations regarding how (how fast, by how much and based on what) these (salary, benefits & perquisites) will change during the employment relationship. Mutual expectations regarding if, when and how these can be (re)negotiated will also be included. We will assume that the 'employer' is represented by the managers of the employee (people in the reporting chain of the employee and also the HR managers).

Salary negotiations happen at multiple points during the tenure of an employee. However, for the purpose of our discussion here, we will conceptualize the same in terms of the salary negotiations at the following stages

1. Before the employee joins the company (when the 'employee' is still an outsider)
2. During the tenure of the employee (from the time the employee joins the organization till he submits his resignation)
3. After the employee submits his resignation (when the company is trying to keep the employee back by making a counter offer)

Let us start with a few basic principles.

When it comes to forming expectations (psychological contract), what was left unsaid can be as important as what was said during the interactions between the employer and the employee. Psychological contract is unwritten, broad and implicit as compared to the employment contract which is written down, specific and explicit. Hence there is much more room for misunderstanding and misinterpretation.

Employees often carry assumptions from their previous employment experiences. Hence, they might assume that something will exist or will not exist in the new organization. Similarly, employers might assume that the new employees will do or will not do something based on the behavior of the current set of employees.

Keeping in mind the above, it makes a lot of sense on the part of both the employee and the employer to surface and validate as many of the possible expectations and assumptions as possible. However, this might conflict with the need to strike a deal quickly. However, any shortcuts employed here can lead to long term pain even if they provide some short-term gain.

The self-image of the employee and the self-image of the manager can have significant impact on the creation and evolution of the psychological contract. Interactions with the colleagues and team members also impact the psychological contract.

When it comes to psychological contract, 'perception is reality'. Breach of psychological contract may occur if employees perceive that the company has failed to deliver on what they perceive was promised. It can also happen when the employer (manager) perceives that the employee hasn't kept his end of the bargain. Usually the issue remains 'underground' for quite a while and by the time it surfaces it would have gained a lot of negative momentum.

Once the breach of the psychological contract occurs, it is often very difficult to repair. Hence prevention is much better than cure in this case!

On the positive side, psychological contract provides an excellent opportunity for the organization to engage with the employees on multiple dimensions - transactional and relational. It can create a deep alignment between the employee and the employer and provide a sense of meaning a purpose to the employees. Hence it makes sense, for both the employers and the employees, to do whatever they can to actively shape and manage the psychological contract!

Salary negotiations before joining

Very few people will disagree with the principle of "a fair day's wage for a fair day's work". But what exactly would be the fair salary for a particular job in a particular company at a particular time (or even what will constitute a fair day's work in the same) is far from simple. This is especially true in the case of those jobs where the employee can influence the results and even shape the job to a large degree based on his capabilities, making the 'fair salary' dependent on the individual.

There are different ways in which fairness can be interpreted by the employer and the employee. For example, when a company is hiring a person should the salary be decided mainly based on the previous salary the person? That is, if the company gives a 'good' (as agreed by the employer and the employee) increase over the previous salary of the new employee, does that indicate a fair deal? What if the salary offered to the employee is lower than that is being paid to other employees in the company (at the same capability level) doing the same job or similar jobs? Can the new employee consider this as an unfair deal? What if the salary offered to the employee is higher than that is being paid to other employees in the company (at the same capability level) doing the same job or similar jobs? Can the existing employees consider that this deal be unfair to them? Should the 'fairness' be decided purely based on the market forces of supply and demand - based on the current market value of the skillset of the employee?

The two basic ways of arriving at the salary for the new employee (entirely based on the employee's previous salary or entirely based on internal equity) are extreme cases. Most companies will do some sort of a balancing act with different companies reaching different 'equilibrium points. For example, most of the companies try to arrive at the new salary based mainly on the previous salary while ensuring that the new salary is within the broad pay range or compensation band for the job (which is market benchmarked). However, these compensation bands are usually quite broad and there is significant room for 'discretion'. Again, it is usually difficult to compare the capability level of the candidate with that of the existing employees and hence both the company and the candidate can make widely differing estimates regarding the relative capability level of the candidate.

Also, there is a basic conflict of interest involved in salary negotiations in most situations – the company wants to pay as a low a salary as possible (while ensuring that the candidate accepts the offer) and the candidate wants to earn as a high a salary as he/she can (while ensuring that he/she gets the job offer).

It is this basic conflict of interest coupled with the different ways of interpreting what constitutes the fair salary for the particular employee that make the interactions between the employer and the employee highly potent from the point of view of the formation of the psychological contract.

During the selection process, the employer and the employee will highlight what each can offer in the prospective employment relationship. This essentially a selling process for both sides and there is always the temptation to oversell and to get a closure as quickly as possible. However, this is key 'moment of truth' (a critical or decisive time on which much depends) in the employment relationship and any statements made during this process (even if it was just a passing mention) is likely to be interpreted by the other party as a promise and give raise to expectations (that form part of the psychological contract).

This is especially true for informal and generic statements that don't find their way into the formal employment contract. For example, if the employer (or any of the agents involved in the selection process like the hiring manager or the HR manager) makes statements like "No one has left us for salary reasons", "In our company there are many people who received multiple salary increases in a year etc. it is highly likely to give raise to (unrealistic) expectations later! Thus, one has to be very careful in making these statements as they are likely to impact the formation of the psychological contract.

However, there is one important advantage at this stage. Since there is no previous history of interactions between the employer and the candidate, there is no existing psychological contract at this stage. Hence while the parties have to be mindful of the impact of the interactions on the formation of the psychological contract, they don't have to worry about the possibility of the interactions violating the existing psychological contract. Hence both the parties can negotiate as hard as they need to do at this stage (a luxury they won't have later). They just need to ensure that they don't say anything that is factually incorrect or misleading.

So, what can we learn from this? There are different ways of interpreting what constitutes the fair salary for the particular employee. I would strongly recommend that the employer explains the process they are using for arriving at the salary in addition to explaining the salary components in detail. Also, if the salary fitment that is being offered has implications for salary progression later (for example, if the salary offered will put the candidate at the top end of the band which will make the future salary increments lower, or if the next increment of the candidate will be prorated as the candidate is joining in the middle of the year) it should be clearly explained. This will enable the candidate to make an informed decision and not to feel like a victim later. Yes, there is a possibility that candidate might not agree with the process and refuses to take up the offer. But this is a much better scenario for both the parties as compared to the scenario in which the candidate joins, feels cheated and leaves the company. Also, broad statements that can get misinterpreted should be avoided.

The candidate should also specifically ask for the process for arriving at the salary and seek clarifications on vague statements made by the employer. Candidates should negotiate as hard as they can at this stage, because trying to renegotiate the salary after one joins the company is a much more complicated process and it could be interpreted as lack of commitment (or 'attitude problem') on the part of the employee and a violation of the psychological contract

Salary negotiations after joining

The salary negotiations that take place during this phase (after the employee joins the organization) are qualitatively different from those during the previous phase (before the employee joins the organization). This is because of the fact that by now a psychological contract has already been formed. The existing psychological contract will have a big influence on the salary negotiations from now on. Of course, the psychological contract can (and does) get modified by the negotiations at this stage. But the changes to the psychological contract at this stage are incremental changes (evolution). Thus, at this stage, the impact of psychological contract on the salary negotiations is much higher as compared to the impact of the salary negotiations on the psychological contact!

In general, the existing psychological contract makes it difficult for the employee to renegotiate the salary – assuming that there is a regular process for reviewing the salaries that is performance linked and market benchmarked. Most of the negotiations happen at this stage because of the 'imperfections' in the previous stage (problems/issues that come up because of the interactions during the phase before the employee joins the organization). For example, if an employee has been promised during the interview stage that that his salary will 'catch up' with that of the existing employees, once he proves himself in the organization and if 'catch up' never happens (or if it takes too long) the employee might feel that his psychological contract has been violated. Organizations should be more careful and specific when they are making such promises (and the prospective employee should seek clarifications or specific details - like how long it will take and what would qualify as proving oneself - if the organization does not do so).

There is another type of violation of psychological contract that can occur. This can be traced to fundamentals of the compensation philosophy of the organization – does the organization pay the employees based on what they deserve (within the constraints of what the organization can afford) or does the organization pay the employees as little as it can get away with? This comes into play in a situation where there is an industry downturn (making it difficult for the employees to change jobs) but the particular organization is doing well. In such a scenario the organization can afford to give the employees good salary hikes. But it can choose not to do so (or choose to give a very low salary hike) because even without the salary hike it can retain the employees.

This certainly provides short term gains. It can also be explained away in terms of salaries being market benchmarked. However, this will violate the psychological contract and will lead to a situation in which the employees (especially very valuable employees) leave the organization as soon as the job market improves (going by the same logic the organization had used, the employees should leave the organization when the market will pay more). No amount of talk about 'employees being the biggest asset' and 'building a great organization together' will undo the damage that happened to the loss of trust.

Another interesting phenomenon observed during this phase is the so called 'entitlement mentality'. This happens when an employee (or a group of employees) feels that he (they) should get a salary hike (or a promotion) because another employee has been given a salary hike or a promotion. While this is usually interpreted as an 'attitude problem' on the part of the employee by many of the organizations, there are significant contributing factors to this from the organization's side.

Often, there is no clearly defined promotion policy or policy/process for 'out of turn' salary increases. When the employees are not clear as to why somebody has been given a salary hike or a promotion (and why they haven't been given the same), they might feel that their psychological contract has been violated. The organization can counteract this to a large extent by having a clearly defined policy for salary hikes and promotions and communicating the same to the employees (and to the prospective employees). Yes, there could be factors related to employee attitudes ('superiority illusion', for example) that are also operating here and they need to be addressed at that level.

Somewhat related to this is the situation where new hires join the organization at a salary higher than that of the existing employees at the same responsibility level. In such a situation the existing employees might feel that their psychological contract has been violated. Unless the organization can clearly demonstrate to the existing employees that there is a valid reason for new hires coming in at higher salaries (for example, they bring in a particular skillset that is not available within the organization and that that skillset enjoys a higher salary level in in the market), this is bound to happen. This situation will also encourage the existing employees (those among the existing employees with skillsets that are highly sought after in the job market) to renegotiate their salaries.

I am not in favour of frequent renegotiation related to the salary. It puts too much strain on the relationship and on the psychological contract. However, in some of the organizations, it might be culturally acceptable to do so and in those contexts the employee might be able to manage this without damaging the psychological contract too much. I have come across organizations where the best paid person is 'a great performer who is always on the verge of quitting'. However, my personal opinion is that this kind of brinkmanship creates mistrust and stress and that it is not worth it from a long-term perspective.

It has to be noted that existing psychological contract also makes it difficult for the organization (represented by its representative like the managers) to reduce the salary of the employees, to be overly demanding or to terminate the employment. A special situation gets created when there is a change in the manager of the employee as the new manager hasn't yet formed the psychological contract with the employee. Usually, the new manager does accept at least some part of the existing psychological contract (or at least what the new manager considers to be the existing psychological contract).

However, if there is a significant leadership change, with many people in the reporting chain of the employee changing, this might not happen (especially if the new set of managers have been brought in to 'transform the organization' and that transformation involves significant changes to the way people are managed in the organization). Thus, the existing employees might feel hassled as they might feel that their psychological contract has been violated and they don't have the opportunity to address the violation. On the flip side, this change in managers/leadership also makes it easier of the existing employees to renegotiate their salaries (at least in the case of those employees who are in a position to negotiate)!

Salary negotiations after resignation

The salary negotiations that take place during this phase (after the employee submits his resignation) are the most complicated ones. One of the key components of the psychological contract in any relationship is the expectations/assumptions about the continuity of the relationship. Here the expectations/assumptions vary widely – across various employees and across various organizations. Hence there is a very high possibility that the expectations (assumptions) the employee have are very different from the expectations (assumptions) that the employer has.

In some organizations, not questioning the continuity of the employment relationship is a necessary condition for any salary negotiations and hence once the employee submits the resignation, the organization does not negotiate at all. Thus, the psychological contract prevents salary negotiations in this case. Other organizations have varying degrees of openness for renegotiating salary/making a counter offer once an employee submits his resignation. However, these negotiations throw up many complicated issues – for both the employee and the employer. The act of submitting the resignation (or not preventing the circumstances that lead to the resignation of the employee) often creates irreparable damage to the psychological contract for the employer and the employee (unless both the parties believe that they themselves were at fault - at least in part - for creating the situation).

If the employer negotiates with employee who has submitted the resignation and manages to retain him/her by making an offer with a higher salary, it might be perceived as a violation of psychological contract by the other employees. Once it becomes known that it is culturally acceptable to submit the resignation and renegotiate the salary, it might encourage other employees to follow suit creating long term damage to the organization culture. Even the employee who managed to get the salary hike might find it difficult to digest that the organization did not recognize his contribution/value till he put in his papers!

It is interesting to note that there is another psychological contract involved in these situations. Since the employee who managed to get the offer from a new organization would have gone through selection process (that would have involved multiple interactions with the organizational representatives of the new organization) his psychological contract with the new organization would also have got formed – at least to some extent. Taking the offer and negotiating with the current employer is usually a violation of that psychological contract!

Another variation of this theme is when an employee resigns from the organization, joins another organization and comes back to the first organization within a short time period with a higher salary and possibly at a higher responsibility level. If this happens in quite a few cases, it can be highly damaging for the psychological contract with the other employees. Hence organizations should have clear norms for rehiring. Keeping all these in mind, my opinion is that salary negotiations after submitting the resignation make sense only under exceptional circumstances.

Rewards or Total Rewards?

Let us start by listening to a conversation between the Rewards Manager and the Organization Development (OD) Manager.

"Compensation decisions are based entirely on the market and business situations. Our objective is to achieve the right balance between 'need to pay' which is based on the market scenario and the 'ability to pay' which is based on the company scenario", said the Rewards Manager.

"Wouldn't that make the rewards function very transactional? Shouldn't you look at the 'want to pay' aspect which is based on the overall people management philosophy of the organization, in addition to the 'need to pay' and 'ability to pay' aspects that you have mentioned?", asked the OD Manager.

"We can't create competitive advantage through compensation strategy as it can easily be copied. Hence, the compensation function has to be transactional and business oriented. While I agree that 'Total Rewards' is our approach, I am only the 'Rewards Manager'. Executing parts of the Total Rewards framework that are not related to compensation and benefits should be the job of the OD function as it is the mandate of the OD function to build a deeper engagement with the employees.", replied the Rewards Manager.

"OD function is also business aligned – it is not about charity and feel-good initiatives. Creating deeper engagement with the organization requires a multi-pronged approach and that includes rewards related dimensions also. Rewards is a very important tool to shape employee behavior. If our rewards strategy is only about 'paying the employees the lowest compensation that we can get away with', we are not only not leveraging the full potential of Rewards, but also creating irreparable damage to the psychological contract between the employee and the employer. Managing the psychological contract is key to building deeper engagement with the employees", said the OD Manager.

My opinion is that both the Rewards and OD Managers here are 'correct' - from the point of view of their respective sub-functions. They are just articulating the mandates given to them. However, while being 'technically correct' they are also missing the essential point here! Please note that one can be 'completely correct' and 'completely irrelevant' at the same time!

So, what should be done? The important thing here (apart from seeing to it that things don't fall through the cracks) is to ensure that there is alignment between what Rewards is driving and what OD is driving.

For example, if OD is working on creating an emotional connect between the employer and the employee (that goes beyond rational commitment) and the Rewards' approach is that 'compensation is purely a matter of supply and demand', then it will send conflicting signals to the employees and also create a violation of the 'psychological contract'.

Let us look at this in a bit more detail. The situation here can be traced back to fundamentals of the compensation philosophy of the organization – does the organization pay the employees based on what they deserve (within the constraints of what the organization can afford) or does the organization pay the employees as little as it can get away with? This comes into play in a situation where there is an industry downturn (making it difficult for the employees to change jobs) but the particular organization is doing well (growing reasonably fast with healthy profits). In such a scenario, the organization can afford to give the employees good salary hikes. But it can choose not to do so (or choose to give a very low salary hike) because even without the salary hike it can retain the employees. This certainly provides short term gains. It can also be explained away in terms of salaries being market benchmarked. However, this will violate the psychological contract and will lead to a situation in which the employees (especially very valuable employees) leave the organization as soon as the job market improves (Going by the same logic that the organization had used, the employees should leave the organization when the market will pay more!!).

A similar situation occurs in the case of hiring also. When the company hires a person (internal or external hire) into a job what salary will be offered? Will the company offer the lowest salary that the candidate will accept or will it offer the salary corresponding to the worth of the job in the company?

At the core, people management is about understanding, predicting and influencing human behavior. Human motivation' is a complex phenomenon. Complex phenomena are usually 'over determined' - that is they have multiple (interrelated) causal/input factors. Some of these factors are in the OD domain and some of the factors are in the Rewards domain. Hence an integrated approach combining Rewards and OD is required. For example, the recent research findings in behavioral economics have created serious doubts on whether many of the performance linked pay schemes have any positive impact on performance. Hence, a combined effort from Rewards and OD is required to ensure a positive return on investment (in monetary and non-monetary terms) from such schemes.

Otherwise, such schemes will just be 'tools to match the pay-out with the ability to pay' - without any useful impact on performance levels.

The paradox of differentiation

The importance of differentiation in people management, including differentiated rewards, is a very popular topic. The matter gets paradoxical when we look at questions like the following: Is differentiation really important? What types of differentiation are relevant? What are the implications of differentiation? Is it worth the trouble and effort?

Now, there are many types of 'differentiation' possible. We can look at differentiation in terms of the parameters on which differentiation is based on (input parameters/criteria) and/or in terms of the ways in which differentiation is implemented (results/outcomes). For example, differentiation can be based on performance, potential, criticality/ impact of the role, job level, job family, market value of the skillset, tenure, business unit etc. or a combination of them. Again, differentiation can be implemented in terms of compensation, incentives, benefits, recognition, career progression, development opportunities etc. or a combination of them.

If we look at the large number of input parameters and outcomes listed above, it becomes apparent that there are a large number of combinations possible here. The relevance of a particular combination will be context specific. To keep this discussion manageable, let us classify the input parameters into three broad categories - parameters that are related most to the

- Individual (performance, potential, tenure etc.)
- Position (criticality/impact of the role, job family, job level, skill set etc.)
- Part of the organization (business unit, function, team etc.)

I must say that these categories are somewhat arbitrary and there could be some amount of overlap among them also. For example, 'skillset' is related to both the role and the individual. It also raises some interesting questions like 'if an employee has a skill that is in the list of 'hot skills' (as defined by the organization) and if the employee is currently in a job that does not need that skill, should the employee be given any sort of differentiated rewards?'.

Based on our classification, the question now becomes whether it makes sense to differentiate based on individual, position or business unit related factors? Different business units in a company might face different markets (both product and factor markets), with different dynamics and market practices. Business units might also differ in terms of their performance and their ability to pay. Hence, there is a strong case for differentiation. However, too much differentiation might lead to a situation where the employees in different business units don't really feel that they are working for the same company! Thus, the organization culture and philosophy become key factors in determining the extent of differentiation. Similarly, it can be argued that some positions in the organization have a much higher impact on organization performance and that some skillsets carry a greater market a higher market value at a particular point, thereby making a case for differentiated treatment. Of course, we should keep in mind the fact that the list of critical positions and the list of key skills can change, sometimes quite quickly.

If we examine differentiation based on individual related parameters a similar argument holds good - higher performance merits higher rewards. The case (if any) for 'tenure' based differentiation usually has more to do with organization culture and values. The case for 'potential' based differentiation (on a standalone basis) is more complex. Anyway, the most common practice is to use a combination of performance and potential. This also leads to interesting situations and challenges.

Now, let us leave aside all these details and examine the core of the issue. I feel that the most important factor driving differentiation related decisions should be 'contribution or value-addition to the organization'. So, if there are some business units, positions or individuals that create relatively more value to the organization, they can be given preferential treatment. By the same logic, the extent of differentiation should mainly be a factor of the variation in the 'contribution or value-addition to the organization'.

While this sounds quite neat and logical, there are a few important prerequisites to make this work. For example, everyone should understand and agree upon what exactly is meant by 'contribution/value-addition to the organization' at the business unit/position/individual levels. We might also need to include probable 'contribution/value-addition to the organization' in the future, apart from the current ''contribution/value-addition to the organization' (differentiation based on 'potential'). Also, it should be possible to track/measure/assess this relative 'contribution/value-addition to the organization', to the satisfaction of everyone involved at all these levels. Again, there should clear norms in staffing the positions and business units to answer the question 'how can I move to that position or unit that gets better treatment'. As we can see, all this can get quite complex.

Similar to what happens when dealing with other paradoxical situations, what really matters the most here is the dynamic interplay of the factors in the particular context. For example, it is worthwhile to aggressively differentiate rewards for 'high-performers in critical job families', if we are in a context where

- Some positions have a much higher business-impact as compared to other positions, and
- In critical positions, a high performer in creates much more value as compared to an average performer

In such a context, such a differentiation can add net business value, even if it can have possible side effects in terms of annoying a large section of the employees who are not part that category. However, if one or more of the conditions mentioned above do not hold good, if they hold good only to a limited extent, the business case for aggressive differentiation becomes less compelling.

CHAPTER 7: PARADOXES IN ENGAGEMENT, BELONGING AND IDENTITY

"I want to do with you what spring does with the cherry trees"

-Pablo Neruda

From the more pragmatic world of rewards, let us move to something more mysterious. The matters related to employee engagement, work identity and the sense of belonging. These become important because they have a big impact on aspects like discretionary effort and the intention to stay. Organizations often trivialize employee engagement, and, sometimes they even try use it as a manipulation tool, to motivate and retain employees without paying them more money.

In this chapter, we will explore some of the paradoxical aspects related to employee engagement, ownership, belonging and work identity. We will begin with a story that can help us to get to the core of employee engagement. Then we will explore the paradoxical issue of the object and subject of employee engagement. We will also look at employee engagement in the special context of restructuring. Next, we will look at the paradoxical aspects related to the sense of ownership and belonging and a manifestation of that in storytelling. This will be followed by the paradox of work identity and then an exploration of the kind of 'passion for work' will be appropriate in the context of today's business organizations.

Employee engagement and the story of the Sky Maiden

"Employee engagement" is one of the popular concepts in organizations these days. Many organizations have launched new initiatives to improve levels of 'employee engagement'. Some of them have dedicated teams to 'handle' this important dimension. I fully agree that 'employee engagement' is very important. There is a lot of research that links higher levels of 'employee engagement' with positive outcomes like improved productivity and reduced attrition rates.

What concerns me is the tendency in some organizations to view 'employee engagement' initiatives mainly as a series of employee communication programmes. Here the term 'employee engagement' gets used in the sense of leaders 'engaging with' or 'speaking to' the employees. Now, this is an important part of employee engagement. The problem is that true 'employee engagement' requires much more than this. Another troubling trend is to equate 'employee engagement' with 'fun and games' activities. 'Fun and games' initiatives are also useful. They provide a temporary distraction from work (especially when they are held during office hours, which sadly is not always the case!). They also provide an opportunity to interact with other employees. But all these do not make any significant change in the basic nature of work or in the work context.

The defining feature of employee engagement is 'discretionary effort' put in by the employees. If employees have to get motivated to put in the 'discretionary effort', just speaking to them and telling them what is happening in the organization (and even just listening to them) won't be sufficient. To get discretionary effort, both the hearts and minds of the employees have to be engaged. Often this calls for interventions to improve the person-job fit, the performance management/rewards system and the organization culture. Of course, it is much easier to hold communication meetings than to ensure that employees are in those jobs that leverage and celebrate their key talents/abilities/interests! But if the objective is to have the type of 'employee engagement' that motivates employees to stay on and to put in discretionary effort, peripheral interventions might not be sufficient.

This brings to mind the 'story of the Sky Maiden'. There are many versions of this story. It goes something like this: Once there lived a young farmer. He used to get up early in the morning every day to milk his cows.

This went on for quite some time. Then he felt that something strange was happening. The cows seemed to be giving less milk than they used to. He tried many methods to improve this situation. But they did not work. Slowly he became convinced that someone was stealing the milk. So, he decided to stay up all night to catch the thief. So, he hid behind a bush and waited. For many hours nothing happened and he was feeling very sleepy. Suddenly he noticed something that left him spellbound. A very beautiful woman came down from the sky and started milking the cows. Initially our young farmer was too dazed to react. Then his anger took over and he managed to catch the thief before she could escape. He asked her who she was and why was she stealing the milk. She told him that she was the Sky Maiden, that she belonged to a tribe that lived in the sky, and that the milk was their only food.

She pleaded with him to let her go. Our young farmer told her "I will let you go only if you promise to marry me". She said "I will marry you. But you need to give me a few days so that I can go back home and prepare for the marriage". He agreed. So, the Sky Maiden left and as promised she returned after a few days. She brought a large box along with her. She said to him "I will be your wife. But you must promise me one thing. You should never open this box. If you open this box, I will have to leave you". He agreed and they got married.

Many months passed. Then one day, while his wife was not in the house, our young farmer could not contain his curiosity anymore and he opened the box. He was surprised to find that he could not see anything in the box. When the Sky Maiden came back, she could sense something was wrong. She asked him "Did you open the box?". He said " I am sorry. I opened the box. But there was nothing in it". The Sky Maiden was heartbroken. She said "I am leaving. I can't live with you any more". He said "Why are you making such a big issue out of this. I told you that the box was empty". She said "I am not leaving you because you opened the box. I knew that you are likely to open it sooner or later. I am leaving you because you said that there was nothing in the box. Actually, the box was not empty. It was full of sky. Before I came to you, I had filled the box with sky which is the most precious thing for me. Sky is the core of my real self. It is what makes me special. It is what makes me who I am. How can I stay with you if you can't even see the thing that is the essence of my Self and that makes me special?"

Now there are many important points here. No deep relationship can thrive unless it recognises and celebrates the factors that define the essential nature of the parties involved and that makes them special. Of course, this is truer for personal relationships and the use of this in a work context is an exaggeration to some extent. But I think that the central point remains valid even in a work context.

The paradox of the object and subject of employee engagement

"You should join us only if you fall in love with our company", said the business leader to a group of summer interns from premier business schools.

"I don't think my exit should be considered as attrition; the company that I am leaving is very different from the company that I had decided to join", said the senior manager during his farewell.

I heard these statements quite some time ago. But they pop up in my mind whenever I think about employee engagement. The first statement, makes me think more about the appropriateness (or the lack of it) of the various metaphors used to describe employee engagement. The second statement makes me wonder who or what exactly is it that the object of employee engagement and if employee engagement is a one-way street. Let's explore these in a bit more detail here.

While there are many definitions of employee engagement, a 'strong emotional connect' that leads to 'discretionary effort' is the central theme in most of these definitions. Also, it is this 'strong emotional connect' that is one of the key underlying factors in the two statements that we started this discussion.

Let's start with the statement of the business leader. He definitely had a point. Any transition to a new organization (especially when it is from campus to corporate) will have its own share of frustrations and if one develops a strong emotional connect to the organization (during the summer training, in this case) it becomes easier to overlook these frustrations. It also helps in not getting distracted at the workplace. The metaphor he used (that of falling in love, in the romantic sense of the term 'love') has remarkable similarities with the 'strong emotional connect' that we found in the definition of employee engagement sense. Yes, romantic love is a great enabler for 'pair formation' (and for recruiting one into the organization). Yes, this type of love can also lead to the employee putting in discretionary effort.

The main problem is that people fall out of this kind of love, that too fairly quickly. To put it in another way, while it is a great enabler for pair formation, romantic love is not so effective when it comes to 'pair maintenance'. Metaphors that are used to talk about the 'employer-employee' relationship often create complications because a metaphor is not an exact comparison and hence inaccurate/misleading meanings and assumptions creep in into our understanding of the relationship. Of course, metaphors have tremendous rhetorical value and hence leaders are tempted to use them for 'motivating' the employees

Falling in love can lead to attachment or even possessiveness which can be counterproductive. Also, if the employee falls in love with the organization (and the organization doesn't fall in love with the employee), it can lead to an exploitative relationship. Love that is not reciprocated often turns into hurt and hate very quickly!

Yes, there are other definitions of love, like the one Scott Peck uses in 'The Road Less Travelled' ('extending oneself for the spiritual growth of another') that can lead to discretionary effort without the complications mentioned above. But, those types of love are not something that someone can 'fall into' as it requires aspects like a higher purpose and conscious decision-making.

This brings us to the interesting discussion on if it makes sense to (re) define engagement as conscious decision that the employees make instead of being an emotional reaction/outcome of emotional connect. While this sounds promising, this type of engagement (which is a deliberate decision) might not so easily lead to discretionary effort if the returns of that discretionary effort (which can very well be in terms of satisfying the higher order needs like esteem or self-actualization in the Maslow's hierarchy in addition to satisfying lower order needs like physiological and safety needs that are usually met by salary and job security).

Yes, I have heard employees making statements like "I keep myself engaged regardless of what the organization does or does not do", though I am not sure if they used the term 'engagement' in the sense of discretionary effort (or just in the sense of keeping oneself focused on one's job). If it is the promised 'magic of employee engagement' (creating something out of nothing, like getting extra work done without paying anything extra for it) that get employers excited about employee engagement, then this definition can create complications!

Now let's come to the statement made by the senior manager. Here the key issue is 'what exactly is the 'company' that the senior manager was referring to when he talked about 'the company he joined' and 'the company that he was leaving'?" Is it the legal entity, is it the company brand, is it the products and product brands, is it the immediate manager, is it the team, is it the senior leaders, is it the CEO, is it some higher purpose (other than making money) served by the company or is it the way get things get done in the company (company culture)? Most of the studies indicate the 'immediate manager' as the most important player in the game of employee engagement. But it could also be because the manager represents the organization for the employee and the organization's 'sins' are often incorrectly attributed to the managers. So, when it comes to the object of employee engagement, there are many possibilities and also many combinations of these possibilities!

If we examine the above list of possibilities (objects of employee engagement), we will find that most them can change and that some of them do change frequently in many organizations these days. This also indicates that the loss of social capital/breaking of working relationships during reorganizations can have an adverse impact on employee engagement.

Again, it is possible that the employee's preferences/factors that engage the employee changes during his tenure in the organization. So, there are many moving parts here, on both sides of the equation, and that makes keeping the employee engaged quite challenging. Hence, employee engagement becomes a continuous activity and it requires a deep understanding and careful management of the evolution of the psychological contract!

At a more fundamental level, the issue here is about the 'reciprocity' aspect of employee engagement. Why is it only about the employees feeling emotional connect to the organization (and putting in discretionary effort) and not also about the organization reciprocating the feeling (and going out of the way to do something for the employees). Yes, as we have seen in the above paragraph, the 'object' of employee engagement can vary and hence the issue of who or what exactly is the 'organization' that is supposed to reciprocate can further complicate things. May be, we can just say that all those who benefit from the discretionary effort put in by the employee should reciprocate. While it is very clear that employee engagement benefits the organization, it is not very clear if it leads to employee happiness or even employee satisfaction in the long run.

So, what does all this mean? To me, (employee) emotions are precious (or even sacred) and they should not be trifled with. Yes, emotions are also highly powerful in driving discretionary effort and they can lead to remarkable (business) results. So, organizations should engage the emotions of the employees only if they are willing to reciprocate (in terms of going out of the way to care for the employees in various ways depending on the context). If the idea is just to increase performance or to create accountability, there are other ways (that works on rational commitment and are well within the scope of the employment contract without getting into the domain of psychological contract) like goal alignment, performance management, gain sharing plans and performance linked incentives that can align the interests of the employer and the employee and hence address the 'principal -agent problem'.

Hence, we should leverage the power of emotional connect (and the discretionary effort that comes from it) only if we are willing to look at employee engagement as a relationship (and hence a two-way street) and are able to consistently respond in a manner that respects and nurtures the relationship! Otherwise, we run the risk of the (perceived) intent of our employee engagement efforts resembling that which is often depicted in the cartoon strips on employee engagement (for example, tricking the employees into 'gladly putting in extra effort without getting paid anything extra in return')!

Of employee engagement and the 'survivor syndrome'

As a special case scenario, let us look at employee engagement in the case of survivors of corporate restructuring/downsizing exercises (who often suffer from the so called 'workplace survivor syndrome' with symptoms like anxiety, depression, decrease in performance, poor morale and increased propensity to leave)

At the heart of the survivor syndrome lies two emotions- guilt ("I didn't deserve to survive when my friends didn't") and fear ("Next time, it could be my turn"). So, when it comes to employee engagement, the organization's best response is to help the survivors to deal with these emotions so that while the scars can't be erased, productivity can be restored to a great extent.

Guilt can be reduced by convincing the survivors that they deserved to survive (by following a transparent process for restructuring and for identifying the employees to be separated, for example) and by ensuring that the employees who were separated have been well taken care of (by providing a generous separation package and adequate transition support, for example).

Fear can be addressed to some extent by publicly communicating (if possible) that the staff cuts have been completed and there is no such possibility in the foreseeable future. Providing the survivors the opportunity to receive psychological counselling/ stress management training with a focus on coping strategies can also help. Of course, constant communication with the employees at all levels that addresses the stated and unstated concerns has to be continued. Another type of fear is regarding increased workloads and new skill sets required. This can be addressed through careful work planning and capability building. People managers can be trained to look for signs of stress in the employees and to manage the employees in a supportive manner. Of course, any tendency among the people manages to use the residual fear to drive productivity ('blackmailing' employees to work harder) should be curbed.

What is perhaps irreversible from the employee engagement point of view (especially for the next few years) is that the employer- employee relationship moves to a purely rational plane (whereas most definitions of employee engagement include the aspect of deep emotional connect that the employees have to the organization). This is because, layoffs are often perceived as a breach of the psychological contract. This would be more so in those organizations that have been communicating messages like 'our company is one big family' to the employees.

This will mean that, after the restructuring, companies will have to rely more heavily on rational means to retain and motivate employees (for example, highly competitive salaries & performance-linked incentives, gain sharing schemes etc.) as well as investment in capability building to ensure 'employability'. Yes, the emotional connect can drive discretionary effort and lead to remarkable (business) results. But organizations should engage the emotions of the employees only if they are willing to look at employee engagement as a relationship (and not as a tool) and are willing to reciprocate (in terms of going out of the way to care for the employees, beyond what the employment contract requires)!

In a way, the way out of the survivor syndrome is through a psychological transition process. So, actions that can facilitate the transition process like clearly explaining the need for restructuring and the process that would be followed, helping the employees to acknowledge and deal with their feelings of fear and guilt (as detailed above), clearly articulating the new vision for the organization and the possibilities it creates for the survivors and getting the survivors actively involved in rebuilding the organization and the social networks within the organization(that would have suffered because of the loss of social capital) are perhaps the highest leverage actions that organizations can focus on!

The paradox of ownership and belonging

"This is as much my company as it is your company", said the Organization Development (OD) Manager when he was having a courageous conversation with the CEO. While he was being deliberately provocative, what he said was factually correct, While the CEO was two levels higher than the OD Manager in the organization hierarchy, the CEO didn't have any other claim to ownership in the company that the OD Manager didn't have.

I do wonder if the OD Manager would have been able to make the same statement, if he was having this discussion with the head of a partnership firm (where the partner is both the owner and the manager) or if he was having the discussion with the CEO of a family-owned firm (where the CEO owns a large percentage of the shares of the company). In a way, this situation is ironic. The role and the mandate of the OD Manager is the same in all the three scenarios. The only difference is that in the second and third scenarios there is someone else in the organization who has an additional claim to ownership that the OD Manager doesn't have. So, the question becomes, just because there is someone else who can say 'My company' in more ways than what you can, does the level of ownership you feel come down?

Let's push this thought experiment a bit more. What if the OD Manager doesn't have any interaction with the CEO and hence there is no way the CEO can convey this message (of having any special ownership claim) directly or indirectly? What if the owner gives up the CEO role and becomes purely an investor but holding the same large percentage of the shares of the company? What if the OD manager is given some shares of the company? Would the risk of the OD Manager feeling less ownership reduce in any of the last three scenarios? Again, if other things remain the same, would there be an impact on the level of ownership based on whether the company in question is a public limited (listed) company or not?

This brings us to the question of what exactly is this 'ownership'. In business organizations, the phrase 'building ownership and accountability among the employees' is heard very frequently these days. To me, accountability is external (you are held accountable by somebody for something and it is usually reinforced with carrot and stick) whereas ownership is internal (it is something you feel). In a way, the relationship between accountability and ownership is similar to that between change (externally imposed) and transition (internal psychological transition that happens in your mind).

It is interesting consider if 'ownership is a conscious decision that you take' or if 'ownership is a feeling that somehow develops in your mind'! It is also interesting to think about what exactly is the object of ownership. Is it your job? your team? your function? your organization or some combination of the above with varying weightages? Yes, the answer can vary for different employees. It can also vary for the same individual across organizations or even within the same organization as one progresses in one's tenure in the organization.

While there can be a difference in opinion on whether ownership is a decision or a feeling, there is agreement on the behavioral manifestation/outcome of ownership. They include taking personal responsibility for the outcomes, going the extra mile, careful use of the resources and even passion for work or the group. These are obviously highly useful to the organization and hence the enormous amount of good press enjoyed by ownership.

In a way, the question of whether your sense of ownership will reduce just because someone else is around who has more claims to ownership is a funny one. It is like asking just because there is someone (nearby or far away) who is more attractive than you, will you feel that you are less attractive as compared what you feel about yourself when you are alone. In another way, this question is not trivial, because the degree of ownership you feel has important implications for your organization (in terms of your productivity on the job) and for yourself (your happiness and satisfaction).

In Economics, this issue of ownership and accountability is represented in terms of the 'principal-agent problem'. The fundamental issue here is the lack of perfect alignment between the interests of the principal (the owner/employer) and the agent (the employee). Hence, the proposed solutions under the 'economics model' are in terms of increasing the alignment by mechanisms like profit sharing, employee stock (option) plans, aligning the objectives of the employee to that of the employer through performance management system backed up by close supervision, performance linked incentives and the threat of termination of employment if the employee actions don't align with what the employer wants. While these have their relevance, they run the risk of (further) shifting the employer-employee relationship to the transaction paradigm away from the relational paradigm and to extrinsic motivation away from intrinsic motivation.

In a way, this makes the contents of the psychological contract very close to that of the employment contract and hence makes the degree of ownership essentially a matter of rational (and not emotional) choice! So, when we operate under this economic paradigm, the organization citizenship behavior (employee behavior that is discretionary/not directly linked to the formal reward system, and that in the aggregate promotes the effective functioning of the organization) and/or extra-role behavior (behavior beyond the role-expectations that can benefit the organization, including whistle-blowing and principled dissent) might take a back seat!

Now, let's look at another type of situation where we use the term 'my'. For example, when I say 'Kerala is my state', what I mean is that I belong Kerala (and not that I own Kerala!). So, ownership can also be about belonging. Another example is that of a 'family'. When I say it is 'my family', I mean that I belong to the family. Of course, if this belonging is sort of 'permanent' it is much easier to accomplish. So, I can say that 'it is my company' also in the sense that I belong to this company, especially if I am confident that this company will continue to be my company for the foreseeable future. Of course, I should also feel that there is a deeper connect between me and the company (in the sense of shared purpose and values), that I have a say in the organization, that I can make a significant contribution to the organization and that I am valued.

This also highlights the power and peril of using the 'family' metaphor in the organization context. If a company uses the family metaphor ('we are all one big family') consistently, it can act as a 'nudge' to the employees to take higher degree of ownership. However, the other associations/assumptions that come with family metaphor (like somewhat unconditional and permanent membership) also gets generated in the minds of the employees. Hence, if the company does a downsizing after that, it will be much more painful (more like a divorce and not just termination of a contract that is economic/transactional in nature) and it is likely to be perceived to be unfair (you don't expect that you will be expelled from your family).

From the above discussion, it is curious to note that in many of the family-owned firms, while there is definitely a risk in creating 'ownership in the sense of possession' (the employees don't own the company and the owner-manager does), it is often compensated by a higher sense of 'ownership in the sense of belonging' (personal connect with the owner and the other employees, long tenures, job security etc.).

Where does this leave us? We can definitely say that ownership need not be in the sense of 'possession'. It can also be in the sense of belonging. Of course, these are not mutually exclusive and they can reinforce each other. Yes, the employees having a high degree of ownership is becoming increasingly important with taking initiative, creativity and discretionary effort becoming ever more critical for business success.

The sense of ownership is experienced in the context of a relationship and a mental model (or paradigm). There are some important aspects of this relationship like empowerment, trust, continuity of the relationship, managing the psychological contract throughout the tenure of the employees etc. Hence, this relationship needs to be nurtured in an ongoing and consistent manner! While the sense of ownership can be beneficial for both the organization and the employee, it often comes with expectations and attachment. Hence, appropriate metaphors should be used, with extreme care, to manage the mental models that govern the employment relationship.

The curious case of the silent organization

"I noticed something surprising during my induction program. While I met many employees from the various functions and levels in the organization, no one told me any stories about the organization. This has never happened to me in any of the organizations that I have worked before!", said the newly hired employee with a puzzled expression.

The first thing that came to mind when I heard the above exchange was the Sherlock Holmes story 'Silver Blaze'. The following exchange takes place in the story:

Scotland Yard detective: "Is there any other point to which you would wish to draw my attention?"

Holmes: "To the curious incident of the dog in the night-time."

Scotland Yard detective: "The dog did nothing in the night-time."

Holmes: "That was the curious incident."

Typically, employees like to tell stories (from the 'glorious past' of the organization) to a newcomer. These stories could be about a great leader who architected a turnaround in the organization, about a team that managed to accomplish a difficult goal in the face of overwhelming difficulties, about something that the organization did that made big impact on the society, about an amazing example of customer service, about a significant innovation or technological breakthrough made by the company, about outsmarting the competition etc. The stories also could be about something in which the employee was personally involved like an accomplishment, a great manager or team member or mentor, an incident where the company went out the way to support the employee during a crisis etc.

Telling these stories to a newcomer allows the employees to 'relive' the incident and feel proud and energized. These stories can help the newcomer to connect to the heart and soul of the organization better than any facts and figures presented during the induction. It is said that a social group (including an organization) constructs its reality through the stories and legends. These stories embody the culture and values of the organization and serve as an effective enculturation tool. Also, the connect between the new employee and the organization (a key component of employee engagement that impacts the motivation and retention of the new employee) happens mainly through the connect the new employee forms with the current employees (and their stories!). So, this kind of storytelling is highly beneficial for the newcomer, the existing employees and the organization.

If these stories are absent, it can be a sign of potential trouble for the organization and a useful 'early warning' for the new employee. Silent or 'story-less organizations' tend to be devoid of 'identity' and 'soul', and, hence it becomes impossible for the stakeholders, including the employees, to connect to it at an emotional level. After all, what is there to connect with?!

Hence, typically, these kind of 'silent situations' occur when the employees are unable to connect emotionally to the organization or when they don't feel proud about the organization, their function or their job. While it is possible that 'nothing worth mentioning has happened in the organization', it is more likely that the employees 'didn't feel the connection and ownership' to what has indeed happened.

These situations are more likely in organizations that take a more transactional approach to people management and don't pay sufficient attention to employee engagement, sense-making and creating a sense of belonging. Another possibility is that the organization has done something trust-destroying (or even 'soul damaging'), like a 'mismanaged restructuring' or 'acting in a manner that very much at odds with the espoused values of the organization'.

The difficult thing here (for the organization) is that the situation can't be remedied just by getting the internal communication function to hunt for/write a large number of stories and do an intense campaign based on those stories. It is because the problem is with the 'emotional connection' to the stories and not with the absence of stories. In a way, it is a like the type of diabetes that occurs not because of lack of insulin but because of the loss of sensitivity to insulin!

At the most fundamental level, this is exactly the way it should be. Storytelling is an intensely human activity and unless the human side of the organization is given adequate importance and nurturing, storytelling (and culture building and employee engagement/retention based on the same) will be an impossible dream!

Stories come alive (for the storyteller and for the listener) only when they come 'straight from the heart' and that can happen only if the employees can connect with the story (and the organization) emotionally (and not just rationally). So, in an organization that doesn't invest in building and sustaining an emotional connect with the employees, employees are unlikely to connect with 'corporate-sponsored stories' and they are even more unlikely to tell those stories to newcomers. Yes, the employees might derive some pleasure in ridiculing the 'corporate-sponsored storytelling' attempt!

I think that storytelling and the connect through the same can take place through virtual interactions also. These days, even psychotherapy is being done effectively through virtual meetings. It has been said that one of the advantages of virtual meetings is that one can observe the other person very closely without making that person feel uncomfortable. Of course, it works the other way around also!

The paradox of job identity

Sometime ago, I left the job that I had been doing for the past few years and took up a different type of job with another organization. I also got the opportunity to take a 3-week break in between. I spent most of this time with some of my close relatives. This also meant that I met a lot people (the friends/relatives of my relatives) - and I was meeting most of them for the first time. One side effect of this was that I had to answer the question "So Prasad, what are you doing now?" - roughly 3 times/day - about 40 times in total, over a two-week period.

Initially, I tried the answer "I am on vacation" - but that did not seem to work. People would wait for me to say more and if I did not say anything more, they would ask me something like "What do you do for a living?". To this I tried to give the answer "I work mainly in the area of Organization Development". But even that answer did not seem satisfactory. Sooner or later people would ask me "Which company do you work for?". To this I tried answering "I am in between jobs" (or "I am taking a break") - but this also did not appear to work well (and sometimes this answer elicited a confused and/or sympathetic look/expression also). So finally, I was forced to answer "I was working for company 'C1' till date ' d1' and I would be joining company 'C2' on date 'd2' ". While this turned out to be 'satisfactory answer' (from a social perspective), I did feel quite uneasy.

My uneasiness was mainly at two levels. At the 'social level' I was bothered about how would I have handled this question if I was not in a position to say that "I would be joining company 'C2' on date 'd2' ". At more personal level, I was wondering whether I can articulate a clear answer (just for my own consumption) to our initial question ("So Prasad, what are you doing now?"), without referring to any of my employers (past, present or future!) or to the job titles. After I thought about it for a while,

I felt that uneasiness at the first level was not a very important - as it was arising mainly from 'social desirability' and 'norms of polite communication in a particular social group' - and hence it should not bother one unduly so long as the 'economic viability' angle has been taken care of. The uneasiness at the personal level was more difficult to address. Once I resisted the temptation to 'destroy the question' by resorting to philosophical answers (like one should be bothered about 'being' as opposed to 'doing'), the real issue became "Have I wrapped my identity too much into my job and career?". I feel that this is an important question that needs to be looked at more carefully.

There are conflicting trends operating here. On the one hand, many of us spend a very large part of our waking lives at work. Many of the jobs are very demanding and they occupy a lot of our 'psychological space' - much beyond office space and office hours. Our 'passion for work', might make work and the achievements at the workplace very important for us. It has also been argued that in an environment where the role holder has the opportunity to shape the role to a large extent (and/or where people are expected to be responsible for managing/developing their careers), role identity and career identity are essential for success/effectiveness. On the other hand, these days many people routinely change jobs or even change careers. Again, often people are forced out of their jobs and careers by organizational changes (right sizing, restructuring etc.). Thus, if your identity is wrapped up in what you do, a change of job or a change of careers (especially if they were forced on you) becomes traumatic (much more so in the case of a job loss).

So where does this leave us? Developing and understanding our identity as individuals is essential for personal effectiveness. This will serve an anchor point for us when everything around us are changing. While job and career identities are useful from a job/career effectiveness/success point of view, they can't define who we are as individuals. Jobs and careers are like the cloths that individuals wear and change. Just as we can't let our cloths define us (though some of us might choose to express some aspects of ourselves through the way we dress), we can't let our jobs and careers define us completely. So, it is very important for one to examine one's current definition of oneself and if the results don't show anything beyond job and career identity, it is time for investing significant time and effort for expanding the boundaries of those definitions. Of course, developing and understanding our identity as individuals is a lifelong process.

By the way, there is another reason for being careful about this 'sense of identity wrapped up in job'. It has been argued that 'sense of identity wrapped up in job' is one of the factors that could predict the risk of violent behavior at the workplace!

The paradox of 'passion for work'

If you have been in the corporate world for some time, it is highly unlikely that you would have been able to avoid hearing statements about 'passion for work'. While most of these statements are made in the context of 'motivational speeches' (without any concrete action points on this 'passion for work'), this is not just a 'philosophical' issue. It has been observed that while 'passion for work' might or might not have a significant impact on actual job performance, 'perceived passion for work' is an important factor in selection decisions. Of course, we have more fundamental issues here - like 'how exactly do we define passion for work' and 'what are the behavioral manifestations of this passion for work'.

While the connection between 'passion for work' and job performance seems logical, I do wonder if one can do anything to develop/enhance 'passion for work' in oneself and/or in others. It appears that it is very difficult to train/'inject'/'program' this 'passion for work' into anyone (including oneself!), especially on a sustainable basis. 'Passion for work' seems to be a by-product of more fundamental things like meaning, purpose, talents, basic personality orientations etc. So, it appears that 'passion for work' is more like something that we can discover/re-discover and help others to discover/re-discover (as opposed to something that we can directly create).

While this seems promising, we might find it difficult to align the 'passion for work' that we have 'discovered' to the immediate job requirements/context - as passion for work might not be bothered about 'minor' things like job descriptions! Maybe, we should 'let our passions find work that meets them' rather than the other way around. Of course, this is not a simple task - either for the individuals (in terms of actually finding such work - over the span of an entire career) or for the organizations (in terms of developing/maintaining the flexibility required - in organization design and in talent management).

It can also be argued that since passion for work is not easily trainable, using 'demonstrated passion for a particular type of work/job' as one of the selection criteria for that job is not a bad idea - especially if we can find a reliable way to define/ assess it (by formulating a definition in terms of its behavioral indicators in the particular context and using behavioral interviews based on those indicators, for example).

Another aspect that intrigues me is the possibility of 'undesirable side effects' of this 'passion for work'. For example, I do wonder if 'passion for work' comes as a package deal - along with complications such as too much attachment to the task/job/position, tendency to attempt for local optima (at the task/individual level results) that might not add up to global optima (at the team and organization level results) etc. On a more philosophical plane, this discussion has similarities with the discussion on the fundamental issue of 'whether happiness and sadness are a package deal' (that is, "can one be 'emotionally open' to feeling happiness while being 'emotionally closed' to feeling sadness?" or "can one reduce one's sensitivity to sadness without reducing one's sensitivity to happiness:").

So, is there a type of 'passion for work' that is does not involve attachment? There does exist such a concept (in yogic literature) - *anasakti*. While *anasakti* is sometimes translated as 'detachment', the true meaning of *anasakti* is closer to 'non-attachment'. Non-attachment is acceptance of situations (and responding to them adequately) without getting emotionally affected by them. This is similar to the ideas of 'being in the world but not of it' and of 'engaging in tasks, yet not being concerned with rewards involved'. It is also interesting to note that *anasakti* has similarities with Scott Peck's definition of true love. A person high in *anasakti* carries out tasks (as a *karma yogi*) with a sense of responsibility and task enjoyment without any additional expectation (while this person does not refuse to enjoy the 'fruits of his labour', he does not get hooked on to these conveniences).

I must say that there is a huge difference between finding the concept of *anasakti* and implementing the same successfully in work-life (as a model of the ideal type of 'passion for work')! Finding a term that describes what we are trying to achieve, does not automatically enable us to achieve it. However, we can get some useful ideas from the thoughts/experience that have already been developed around the term (though in a slightly different context) and this in turn might help us avoid 'reinventing the wheel' in some aspects. So, our quest for finding and implementing the ideal type of 'passion for work' continues.

CHAPTER 8: PARADOXES IN THE BIG PICTURE - VISION, MISSION, VALUES AND CHANGE

It is the stretched soul that makes music, and souls stretched by the pull of opposites.

-Eric Hoffer

Having explored the aspect of engagement and belonging, let us look at the broader picture in organizations that are key enablers for finding meaning and purpose at work. For most of us, work is as much about finding the daily meaning as it is about finding the daily bread. This brings us to the domain of the Vision, Mission and Values of the organization. With the increasing amount of flux in the environment, another big picture theme that throws up a lot of paradoxes is that of managing change.

Vision is a snapshot of the preferred future. Mission is the purpose of the organization and the reason for its existence. Values are what the organization considers as important.

Let us look at some of the paradoxes in this domain. First, we will investigate a strange phenomenon – that of vision statements perpetually remaining in the future. Vision and mission are typically mentioned together. We will explore if this has to be necessarily so. After that we will move to the interesting domain of values and explore some of the paradoxical aspects related to values. Finally, we will explore the contradictions related to change and progress in business organizations, and the issue of 'passive resistance' that is often cited as a key impediment to driving change.

The strange case of the Sublimation of Vision Statements

A vision statement provides a snapshot of the preferred future of the organization. Usually, a timeline is attached to the vision statement ('By

2025, we will be the largest company in our industry by revenue', for example)

Sublimation is the name for the phenomenon when a substance changes directly from the solid state to the gaseous state without going through the liquid state (so we are using the 'Chemistry' meaning of 'sublimation' - as opposed that in 'Psychology')

So how do these two apparently unrelated concepts come together? Vision statements have this interesting tendency to move directly (sublimate!) from 'future' to the 'past' without bothering to go through the 'present'!

In practical terms, what happens is something like this. In 2015, a company sets up a 2020 Vision. Around 2018 or 2019 the same company replaces the 2020 vision with a 2025 Vision. Once this 2025 vision is in place, the 2020 vision is discarded and company is no longer bothered about seeing if the company achieves the 2020 vision. So, the 2020 vision directly moves (sublimates!) from the 'future' to the 'past' without bothering to go through 'present' reality! Hence, 'future becomes a great place to hide' the lack of progress on working towards the Vision!

While this sounds like 'cheating', it might not be that harmful to the organization. Vision, as opposed to a goal, is meant to be aspirational. It can even be argued that calling a long-term aspiration as 'vision', and thereby putting it on a pedestal (and following it too rigidly), can in in fact be harmful to the organization in a rapidly changing environment as it might hinder the organization from seizing emerging (unanticipated) opportunities.

Hence, in a way, it makes sense to keep the vision perpetually (and safely!) in the future. Ultimately, what the employees want is a sense of direction and purpose and not vision statements!

The paradox of Mission without Vision

Recently, I tried to do some sort of 'life planning'. Conditioned by the two decades spent in the management domain, my first impulse was to try to write out mission and vision statements for myself.

When I tried to do this, something interesting happened. I was able to write the mission statement very easily. But somehow, I couldn't write the vision statement!

This surprised me quite a bit. Usually, mission (purpose) and vision (snapshot of the preferred future) go together. Then why am I able to write the mission statement so easily but not the corresponding vision statement?

What deepened the mystery was that when I had attempted to write my mission and vision statements a decade ago (as part of a training program that I was attending) I didn't face any such difficulty in writing a vision statement. This left my wondering what happened during the intervening decade that made writing the mission statement much easier and writing the vision statement much harder.

May be, what is happening is that I am becoming increasingly aware of the unpredictable nature of life. I have realized that fixed definitions of success can become more of constraints than enablers - not only what you planned for doesn't come through but also you miss out on other (sometimes 'better') opportunities because you were not open to them.

So, a mission (which is more like a compass) fits in much better with this dynamic scheme of things as compared to a vision (which is more like a static picture of the preferred future)! Of course, one can set goals so long as the goals don't make oneself not open to the emerging new/better possibilities that are in alignment with one's purpose(mission). As opposed to goals, visions tend to me more permanent (and with a longer time frame or without a specified time frame). So, the problem is only with putting a 'picture of success' on a pedestal and adding unnecessary rigidity to it by calling it a vision.

Life experience often gives you clues on 'who you are' by showing you 'who you are not'. Of course, life experience also gives you clues on 'what you are designed to do' and 'what is important to you'. This definitely helps in sharpening one's understanding of one's purpose (mission) and that is probably why I was able to write my mission statement much more easily this time (and felt it to be more accurate).

The paradox of values and competencies

"If we don't clearly differentiate between values and competencies, we are devaluing the values!", said the Organization Development Manager to the HR Business Partner. They were discussing the plight of the new hires in the organization who were confused by similar-looking names that they come across in the list of organization values and in the competency framework of the organization. Since this is quite a familiar situation across organizations, let's try to explore the domains of values and competencies in a bit more detail here.

To begin with, let's understand these two concepts more deeply. Competencies are a combination of knowledge, skills and attitudes that lead to success/superior performance (in a job, in a function or in an organization) Values are the things that the organization 'values' (considers to be important) and hence values are deeply-held beliefs about what is most important.

Most of the confusion comes because we often don't take the organization values seriously. In many organizations, they are an ornamental piece (that is, they don't really influence decision-making) and they harmlessly exist in the posters on the walls of the organization and in the slides of PowerPoint Presentations (typically in the elite company of the vision and mission statements of the organization).

To me, something should be called a value only if it is so important (so valuable and so core to the organization) that it would be exhibited even if it leads to competitive disadvantage or even a loss for the organization. Since competencies (by definition) are linked to success, this clearly brings out the difference between competencies and values. In a way, competencies are about how to win and values are about how to live, and winning has to be done within the overall context of living!

The difference between values and competencies are evident in the typical manner in which they are arrived at. Competency frameworks are 'designed' where as values are 'discovered' or 'crystallized'. In a way, competencies are more a matter of the mind where values are essentially a matter of the heart!

Typically, values are identified at the organization level (that is, there is only one set of values for the organization) whereas competencies can be defined at job, function and organization level (based on what leads to success at each of the levels). Competencies are developed whereas values are aligned! Addressing competency gaps in the employees is much easier as compared to addressing lack of alignment between the values of the employees and the values of the organization.

The competency frameworks are often revised much more frequently (based on changes in business environment and strategy) as compared to the values for the organization. It is interesting to note that the organization values are often a reflection of individual values the founding members of the organization. While the values of the organization can be shaped to some extent by the members of the organization and by significant events that shape the organization over a period of time, values remain relatively more stable as compared to competencies. The relative stability of values is also because the fit between the individual values and the organization values (the so called 'culture-fit') is often a criterion in the selection process! In a way it makes sense, as inculcating values is a long process!

It is interesting to note that while the same thing can be a competency or a value, the implications are vastly different. For example, if 'customer orientation' is a competency, we will probably understand customer needs deeply and meet the needs better that what our competitors do so that the customer is willing to pay us more. But if 'customer orientation' is a value, we will meet a commitment made to the customer even if it leads to a loss for the company (even when there are ways to wriggle out of the commitment). So, while values might look nice and innocuous, they definitely need skin in the game!

Competencies should be exhibited in the context (spirit and boundary conditions) provided by the values! If this condition is met and the difference between values and competencies are clearly understood, then the same thing ('customer orientation', for example) can be both a value and a competency in an organization and it might even be beneficial as it might lead to greater focus on capability building (as competencies are often linked to HR processes like assessments and learning & development).

Yes, deeply-held values can guide behavior when no one is looking (and even shape how we experience and interpret the world) and values can be a great culture-building tool (In a way, culture is encoded in the DNA of values!). But if there is a disconnect between the espoused values and the enacted values, it will lead to confusion and loss of trust that can be very damaging to the organization culture. Technically speaking, it can be argued that values are 'value-neutral' (in the sense that what defines them is their supreme importance to the group and not their correctness according to some external ethical standards). But we must remember that each group is part of a larger society and there are some basic standards of ethics that are largely accepted by most of the current human populations!

So, what does all this mean? I am all for leveraging the power of values so long as the values are really valued. That is, we should include something as a value if and only if it is so important to us that if required, we will be prepared to take a hit to the business for it. This conflict is easier to manage if the values are in sync with the core purpose of the organization. Actually, some companies include values explicitly in the purpose/mission statement (as opposed to keeping it separate). Of course, this will work only in those organizations where the purpose/mission of the organization is taken seriously!

Identifying the values is only the first step. After that entire chain of activities including clearly describing the values and articulating why values are so important, creating and communicating representations/examples of how each of the values play out in the various parts of the business, ensuring that the leaders visibly demonstrate the values/are role models in living the values, conducting values workshops across the organization to enable the employees to understand what exactly each of the values mean in the context of their jobs so that they can live the values more completely in their jobs, collecting and celebrating/recognizing outstanding demonstrations of the values across the organization, measuring the actual experience (of lack of it) for the values across the organization and taking action to reinforce the values where needed etc. begins! Of course, we must validate that the policies and processes in the organization are in alignment with the organization values.

How strongly a value is held decides the extent to which it influences decision-making. Also, if there are multiple values, how strongly each one is held becomes the deciding factor when there is a situation where the values are in conflict (that is, where we have to prioritize one value over the other). Since values usually 'goody-goody things', often we don't even consciously think about the relative importance of the values to us, unless we are forced to choose between values (and hence the importance of doing an exercise like 'value auction' that forces us to prioritize the values as part of value clarification/crystallization sessions). It is also highly useful to clearly articulate (during the values workshops mentioned above, for example) how to deal with situations where there is a possible conflict between two of the company values!

Hence, while values are very powerful and useful, they also involve hard decisions and hard work! So, 'handle with care'!!

The paradox of change and progress

Whenever I think about the paradox of change and progress, the first thing that comes to mind is a 'kaizen story', that I heard a long time ago. A particular organization had rolled out kaizen (continuous improvement). An incentive scheme was also launched to reward the employees who make any such improvement in any part of work. So, one person successfully claimed a 'kaizen' for putting some flowerpots in the work area and thereby 'improving the work environment'. After sometime, another person successfully claimed a kaizen for removing those flowerpots and thereby 'improving the flow of people and materials in the work area'. So, we were back to square one though it counted as two kaizens (making the organization appear 'continuously improving') and both the employees received their incentive pay-out!

While the above story might come across as a caricature (and not a portrait) of what actually happens in business organizations, it has more than a grain of truth. One of the reasons why this story connects so well is that it almost perfectly matches the definition of a 'myth'. A myth is a story that keeps on happening again and again in various forms, because it contains a deep truth (a deep truth about the nature of reality in organizations, in this case)!

The biggest source of waste in many business organizations, that so deftly escapes even lean six sigma and productivity improvement efforts, is that results from frequent changes in direction and the tendency to equate 'change' with 'progress'. Yes, rapid changes in direction, including fast U-turns, helps in creating some sort of illusion (or even a convenient collective delusion of) progress and of taking 'decisive action'.

The point here is not that one shouldn't change the direction when it is required or that one shouldn't correct one's mistakes. Constantly making micro-adjustments as the situation evolves is very much part of the paradoxical thinking approach. The point here is just that one should be mindful of and take some accountability for one's decisions, and the organization and human costs associated with those decisions!

The paradox of 'passive resistance'

"There is too much passive resistance in this organization! When I suggest something, everyone agrees. But they go back and do whatever they wanted to do", said the frustrated business leader.

'Passive resistance' is a term that is heard quite often in business organizations. Let us begin by taking a look at this phenomenon from a broader perspective.

From a psychological point of view, passive resistance is a form of passive-aggressive behavior. Passive-aggressive behavior involves acting indirectly aggressive rather than directly aggressive. It usually manifests as procrastination, resentment, sullenness, helplessness or even as deliberate failure to accomplish tasks.

From a socio-political perspective, passive resistance is a method of nonviolent protest against laws or policies in order to force a change or secure concessions. This involves methods like economic or political non-cooperation, hunger strikes, mass demonstrations, refusal to obey or carry out a law or to pay taxes, economic boycotts, symbolic protests etc.

Keeping these in mind, let us come back to passive resistance in the context of business organizations. Employees exhibiting 'active resistance' are vocal in their criticism and they might even make efforts to cause the change to fail. Employees showing 'passive resistance' exhibit little visible resistance. They will outwardly agree with the change that is being proposed, but then act as if they don't. Though they don't challenge the change directly, they will continue doing things their own way.

The typical behavioral manifestations of passive resistance in organizations include

- Not taking ownership while appearing to agree with the proposed change
- Diminished enthusiasm, withdrawal, sulkiness, apathy, cynicism or hopelessness
- complaining without offering solutions
- Blaming others
- Indecisiveness and procrastination
- Excessive adherence to procedures and guidelines
- Working inefficiently or making half-hearted efforts
- Withholding information
- Forgetting obligations and commitments
- Repeatedly making excuses to avoid assigned tasks
- Working on unnecessary tasks

- Over-complicating the new way of working
- Propagating rumours

From these it appears that passive resistance is clearly something 'bad'. So, what is paradoxical about passive resistance? As we have seen earlier, a paradox occurs when there are multiple perspectives that exist alongside, each of which is true, but they appear to be in conflict with one another. Now, let us look at some of the opinions about passive resistance

- Passive resistance is more dangerous than active resistance as it is a 'silent killer' (that goes undetected and hence unresolved).
- People who display passive resistance lack the courage to stand up for what they believe in.
- People resort to passive resistance to hide their incompetence.
- The primary reason for passive resistance is an environment where the direct expression of disagreement is discouraged. When employees feel that they cannot express their opinions and emotions openly, they might resort to more indirect methods of expressing the same.
- Passive resistance can be a very 'logical response' in a hierarchical organization where it is culturally unacceptable to oppose the views of the superiors directly.
- It is often the 'good' employees (highly independent, highly competent and highly committed) who exhibit passive resistance. They are the people who can operate with a high degree of independence (a very valuable capability in rapidly evolving business organizations). Their high degree of competence enables them to realize that the plan of action suggested by the superiors might not always be correct or in the best interest of the organization. They also care too much about their work and the organization to just 'go along'. Again, they are intelligent enough to realize that they can't express their disagreement directly without seriously jeopardizing their careers. Hence, they respond with passive resistance!

- Sometimes, passive resistance can be a 'rational' behavior which lets an employee dodge unnecessary tasks while avoiding confrontation. Employees often resort to passive resistance when the assigned task/imposed view does not 'make sense' to them. It helps the employee to gain a sense of control. Passive resistance becomes problematic only when it becomes a habitual and indiscriminate response.

- An employee might not always be consciously aware of his/her passive-aggressive behavior.

- The basic 'animal response' in a stressful situation is 'fight' or 'flight'. 'Fight' is similar to active resistance and a fight response (in its basic form) might not be a possible (without serious repercussions) in many situations that employees face in business organizations. Similarly, a 'flight response' in its basic form (for example, getting out of the situation by changing roles or changing jobs) might not also be feasible. Hence 'passive resistance' (which can be conceptualized as a 'creative' combination of 'fight and flight') becomes a 'natural response' to cope with the brutal realities of organizational life. By the way, it has been argued that insanity is a perfectly sane response to an insane environment!

Please note that the attempt here is not to glorify (or even to justify) passive resistance. The idea is to develop a richer understanding of the paradox that underlies the phenomenon of passive resistance, in order to respond to passive resistance more effectively.

So, how should we deal with passive resistance- in ourselves and in others? A good place to start is to examine some of the causes of the passive resistance mentioned above.

If the cause for passive resistance is an environment where the direct expression of disagreement is discouraged, the logical first step should be to make it more safe/acceptable to express opinions/disagreement more directly/openly. Of course, this is easier said than done, changing (hierarchical) cultures often requires significant amount of time and effort.

If the passive resistance is based upon the belief that past practices have been sufficient and there is no need to change, then placing more emphasis on creating and communicating the 'business case' for the change becomes critical. This is especially important in those situations, where employees go into passive resistance as a means of retaliation for some decision or action, which they perceive to be unfair or unjustified.

If the key contributing factor is lack of lack of competence or lack of confidence in their ability to execute, then capability building & coaching should be looked at.

If the problem is primarily with the loss of control/independence, getting the employees more involved in the change process, giving them more freedom in determining how to carry out the task and reducing the amount of micromanagement (while ensuring accountability) will help.

If the main contributing factor is some sort of 'learned helplessness', enabling people to examine their thought processes (and the inferences/attribution errors they are making) along with enabling them to build the requisite skills to operate in the new environment will help. If the transition from 'learned helplessness' to 'learned optimism' can be facilitated, it would provide a significant advantage when it comes to dealing with the next wave of change.

Hence, the primary strategy to deal with passive resistance is to surface it so that it can be addressed in a reasonable manner. However, if there are issues at the structure level (administrative and functional managers of an employee driving conflicting priorities in a matrix organization, for example), at the group level (inter-group conflict, for example) or at the interpersonal level that led to passive resistance down the line, they need to be addressed at the appropriate level. Of course, basics of good change management like articulating the vision, communicating the business case for the proposed change and the 'what is in it for me' for the impacted individuals, creating forums to raise and address issues, demonstrating top management commitment and helping employees to improve their change resilience are very much relevant here also.

CHAPTER 9: PARADOXES IN LEADERSHIP AND FOLLOWERSHIP

It is a terrible thing to look over your shoulder when you are trying to lead and find no one there.

-Franklin Roosevelt

Leadership is an evergreen topic. Though we have a huge number of books and articles in in this domain, the rate at which new books and articles on leadership are coming out is not slowing down in any way. Similarly, Leadership Development is a multi-billion-dollar business. Why should there be so much noise and investment related to what should be a natural human activity?

One of the key reasons for this is that the concept of leadership is inherently paradoxical. There as many views on leadership as there are people who think about leadership!

The high mindshare that leadership gets is also because we often want to look at leaders as magical people with superpowers who can make the fortunes of the organization turn around. Yes, by virtue of their position they can do both great harm and great good to the organization and the employees.

Leaders in business organizations have to balance multiple priorities that are often in conflict with one another. Because of the paradoxical nature of leadership, when a leader tries to solve a particular problem, he/she often creates new problems that needs new solutions. Similarly, even after a problem is solved, it might not remain solved as the context changes.

In this chapter, let us look at some of the paradoxical aspects of leadership, starting with the polarities of leadership. We will begin by exploring the polarities of leadership and then look at some aspects of leadership that are particularly intriguing. When new leaders come into an organization, they are often unable to be effective in the new organization. We will explore the paradoxical aspects of leadership transitions and develop some pointers what can be done, by the organization and the newly hired leader, to make the transition successful.

The polarities of leadership

To me, leadership is primarily about achieving the optimal balance between the various polarities in organizational life.

You are a leader if you can find the right balance between polarities like

- Being confident and making a vulnerable connection
- Providing hope and being realistic
- Driving change and maintaining stability
- Shaping the organization culture (and the definition of 'good' in the organization) and adjusting to the organization culture
- Taking too much risk and taking too little risk
- Employee needs & organization needs
- Focusing on the long term and responding to immediate challenges
- Taking charge and letting others take charge (control and autonomy)
- Maintaining a broad perspective and developing micro-awareness
- Being consistent and being flexible
- Transparency and confidentiality
- Organization building and creative destruction
- Acting based on who you are as an organization and acting based on what the environment demands
- Holding on and moving on

The 'right balance' is highly context specific. It is also a dynamic balance/equilibrium as opposed to a static one (In a state of static equilibrium there is balance, but no change or movement - that exists in the case of dynamic equilibrium. For example, a chair has static equilibrium while a bicycle in motion has dynamic equilibrium). Again, the equilibrium point is an evolving one - based on the evolution of the leader, followers and the organization.

All in all, it is quite a moving target & that is why it is so difficult to 'train in' leadership. While useful inputs/helpful experiences/coaching can be provided, leadership capability emerges in a non-linear fashion in the being of a person based on years of struggle with the polarities mentioned above! Of course, all the organizational issues are not 'polarities' and one of the necessary conditions for leadership to emerge is the ability to differentiate between 'a polarity to be managed' & 'a problem to be solved'!!

Since we have defined the work of leadership in terms of 'achieving optimal balance between polarities in organizational life', it will be interesting look at this 'optimal balance' in more detail. It is not about 'compromise' between the two poles (like a consistent score of 3 in a 1 to 5 scale-with 1 representing one pole and 5 representing the other). It is more about being a '1', '2', '3', '4' or '5' based on the situation. Strangely, it also involves transcending the scale by (as Pirsig says) catching the bull (polarity) by both its horns (poles) & even singing the bull to sleep.

It is not about being 'timid' and avoiding strong decisions/behavior. It is about the ability to display a wide spectrum of responses and the courage to choose the appropriate response based on the situation. The courage also involves the willingness to explain why a particular choice was made in a particular situation - so that the behavioral flexibility won't become confusing to the team (that is, variation in responses has to be accompanied by consistency at the level of underlying principles of choosing particular responses in a particular situations & these principle have to be communicated to the team - otherwise this flexibility will come across as inconsistency). Yes, this also involves taking feedback/admitting one's mistakes and revising one's mental map when required. Deep understanding & trust about the leader (that is, understanding 'who he is' in terms of the principles governing his actions) - developed over a period of time - will obviate the need to explain everything every time! It is said that 'sometimes, who you are speaks so loudly that people can't hear what you are saying'!

Developing this kind of behavioural range, that too across the many polarities in organizational life, takes a lot of development (psychological/spiritual growth) on the part of the leader. Please note that displaying a wide range of behaviours can put a lot of pressure on the leader's psyche as it involves 'holding multiple sets of diametrically opposite ideas in the mind at the same time' and constantly adjusting the balance (as it is about dynamic balance as opposed to static balance). Yes, this development/growth (like all psychological growth) can be taxing as it demands regularly stretching one's boundaries. No -this does not mean that there is no room for the natural self/style of the leader, as it is about expanding the self as opposed to developing towards some (standard) 'ideal self'. Yes - it usually takes significant amount of time. But we need to keep in mind that this development is a matter of degree & that different people learn at different speeds. So, investing in increasing one' ability to 'derive learning/growth from experience' becomes critical - especially for young leaders!!

The 'Leadership Sandwich'

If we look at the terminology used in business organizations, often there is a level called 'Team Leader' that appears just above that of a Team Member but below that of a 'Team Manager' or 'Project Manager'. Beginning with the Team Manager/Project Manager level, there are multiple levels of 'Managers'. But after these 'managerial levels', 'Leaders' (Business Leaders) again make an appearance. So, we have a curious situation - we have managers 'sandwiched' by leaders. Hence the 'leadership sandwich' occurs.

I was wondering why this 'leadership sandwich' occurs. Why do we have levels/roles with the term 'Leader' in the title on both the sides of the levels/roles with the term 'Manager' in the title? Since too much have already been written about the 'Leaders Vs. Managers debate', I have no intention to get too deep into that tricky territory. But these kind of 'sandwich' situations interest me immensely, because I feel that some phenomenon similar to that of the 'U-curve' in Anthropology might be operating here. In such cases, something starts in one state, moves to the opposite state, and then comes back to the original state at a higher plane (creating a 'U' - shaped pattern). Hence, I was wondering if 'Leadership' also follows such a 'U' - shaped pattern!

Maybe, we can get a clue to the (leadership sandwich) puzzle if we compare the role of a Team Leader with that of a Team Manager. Typically, a Team Leader does not have formal authority (that is, to hire, fire, evaluate and reward staff). Therefore, a Team Leader is forced to influence (get the work done) without formal authority. Team Managers (and the multiple levels of Managers above them) do have formal authority.

Of course, the 'Leaders' who are at higher levels as compared to these 'Managers' also have formal authority - much more than what these 'Managers' have. But maybe these senior 'Leaders' are supposed to influence (get the work done) without exercising their formal authority, though they do have a lot of formal authority. Maybe they are supposed to do the influencing in 'better/higher ways' (for example, by creating an inspiring vision, by building a high-performance culture etc.). Hence, if we can say that "Team Leaders influence without formal authority because they don't have any formal authority and Business Leaders influence without formal authority because they choose not to exercise their formal authority", then we have the description of a phenomenon that follows the U-curve perfectly!

Leadership or Manipulation?

It can be argued that all the leadership actions involve influencing and hence some element of manipulation, as it involves getting a person to do something that he/she would not have done otherwise. Now, the question if this manipulation is for a 'good' cause (and for whose 'good') will bring us close to the domain of ethics, and the tricky terrains of situational ethics vs. code ethics, individual good vs. collective good, good of one collective vs. good of another collective etc.

If the leader gives me some information that opens my mind (by enabling me to see some possibilities that I was not able to see before, for example), I might get inspired, and do something that I might not have done otherwise. But if the leader gives me the additional information selectively, so that I will see only those new possibilities that he/she wants me to see (so that I will take some particular action, for example) then the element of manipulation creeps in. Yes, the line between 'influencing and manipulation' can indeed be a very fuzzy one!

The paradox of 'thought leadership'

Thought leadership has been a very popular concept for quite some time. The beauty of this concept is that anyone can declare himself to be a thought leader as no formal authority or reporting relationship is required to be a thought leader. This raises an interesting question: "Can leadership, including thought leadership. exist without followers?"

The answer will depend on the definition of leadership. My preference these days is to think about leadership as an emergent phenomenon that takes place in the context of a relationship or in the context of a set of interactions. Going by this definition, leadership cannot without followers unless 'leading oneself' is considered to be a leadership activity.

Attempting 'thought leadership' in these areas related to people management has interesting implications. It will not be feasible to prescribe effective standard or algorithmic solutions that can apply to a wide range of contexts in this domain. The kind of thought leadership that is likely to be useful here will be more in terms of providing a new perspective, deepening the richness and understanding of the paradox, providing an experience that provides empathy, hope and amusement to the people grappling with the paradox etc.

It can also be inferred that this kind of thought leadership need not involve providing any sort of 'answers'. It can exist purely in the form of providing new questions that will help others to see the problem/paradox in a new way, enhance their understanding, and trigger solutions in their mind. Thus, the purpose of thought leadership in this domain will be to trigger solutions in the mind of people dealing with the paradoxes as opposed to prescribing solutions directly.

Followership behaviours of leaders

A few years ago, I got an opportunity to attend a 'global HR leadership team meeting'. This meeting brought together senior HR leaders of the company from various countries and from the corporate office. Though the main purpose of my participation in the meeting was to lead a working session (on an initiative that I was managing at that time), it also gave me a great opportunity to observe the HR leaders of the company for three days.

What struck me the most was the 'followership behaviours' of some of these leaders (that is, their behavior pattern when they are interacting with leaders who are even more senior than them). In quite a few cases this was very different from their behavior in those situations where they were the senior most person present. The supreme confidence and aggressiveness that were often present in their behavior in the latter case were completely absent when they were in the presence of leaders who are more senior than them. Initially, this difference caused some amount of 'dissonance' in my mind. But it helped me to develop a more realistic and balanced understanding of these people as individuals and also of their degree of power/influence/importance in the organization. This proved to be very helpful in working more effectively with these leaders later.

I do wonder how much difference is there between the 'leadership' and 'followership' behaviors of most people. Maybe, we can say that the difference is there in the case of most people. Of course, this difference is a matter of degree and in the case of some of the leaders there won't be a significant difference in the behavior. It might also be that the difference will be more in the case of more hierarchical organizations and in the case of more 'authoritarian leaders'.

An even more interesting question is whether it is 'OK' to have a difference between one's 'leadership behavior pattern' and 'followership behavior pattern'. I feel that some amount of difference is 'normal', in the statistical sense of the term (that is, fitting into a normal distribution). I do feel that a very high degree of difference (resembling 'split personality') is not desirable, especially when the difference in behavior is used to manipulate one's subordinates and/or superiors.

All of us are leaders and followers. It can be argued that 'leadership' and 'followership' are present in all of us and that one of them ('leadership' or 'followership') becomes 'active' in a particular situation. This leads to some interesting questions. To what extent is 'leadership' and 'followership' a choice of the individual concerned? Is this always a conscious choice? To what extent does the situation influence this choice? If we treat leadership as an 'emergent phenomenon', can one do anything to improve one's chances of 'emerging' as a leader?

The paradox of making successful leadership transitions

"Our approach has been to bring in new leaders who can take the company to the next level of excellence", said the Business Leader. "Are we sure that those new leaders have performed better than the existing leaders?", asked the Organization Development (OD) Manager*.

Infusing new talent across levels, especially at leadership levels, has been a favourite response of many organizations, when faced with performance or organization effectiveness challenges. There is definitely some merit to this. If the existing leaders have failed to meet the organization goals, they might be part of the problem. Sometimes, the existing leaders don't have the requisite skills or experience to drive business transformation, especially when the business is moving into new domains.

It is also true that a business leader can't micro-manage a large organization and hence has to depend on the leaders down the line. Again, there is no point in hiring highly capable leaders and giving them micro-instructions on what exactly they should do. However, this strategy is not as simple to implement as it appears to be!

Yes, it is highly tempting to just 'throw new people at problems or opportunities'. Replacing existing leaders with new leaders sends strong messages both inside and outside the organization. It can create the perception that the organization is taking 'decisive action' and that the future is likely to be much better than the present.

So, what is the problem with this approach? To begin with, it often happens that problems at the organization strategy, structure or policies level get misdiagnosed as individual capability issues of leaders down the line. If that is the case, unless the new leaders have the empowerment to change/influence those upstream issues (at organization strategy/structure/policy levels), they have no chance of being successful. If the failure of new leaders also gets (conveniently) diagnosed as 'hiring mistake', this cycle of 'hiring - firing - hiring' new leaders will go on! Of course, if the new leaders also follow the same philosophy and bring in new people to their teams, this can snowball into large number of people changes with the associated disruption/ripple effects (and an absolute bonanza for recruitment consultants). All this can create an illusion of progress.

The organizations that have a propensity to make leadership changes at the slightest provocation might also be prone to a 'swim-or-sink' attitude ('now that you have been hired as a leader, it is up to you to make it work') once the new leaders join the organization -with not enough emphasis given to new leader assimilation and to putting in place the supporting structures for new leaders (sufficient investment of time by senior leaders and mentors, for example). This can get further complicated if the new leader doesn't get the required resources, he/she needs. Of course, leaders are expected to 'do more with less'. But 'creating something out of nothing' is more like magic and not management. Similarly, the degree of stretch in the role might not be realistic. It is important to differentiate between 'stretch roles and designed to fail roles'!

Now, it would be unfair to say that all the failures in leadership transitions are the fault of the organizations. There are many things the newly hired leaders can do to make an effective transition. Let's look at just four of them and also explore what can be done jointly by the newly hired leader and the organization to maximize the possibility of a successful transition.

Validate 'what good looks like': Individual leaders have personalities, values and work preferences. Organizations have their own preferred ways of doing things, behavioral norms and underlying assumptions ('culture'). A large degree of alignment between the leader's and the organization's underlying definitions of 'what good looks like' would make life easier for both the parties and enhance the chances of a successful leadership transition. There are two specific actions that can help here. The first is ensuring a more in-depth and open discussion on the 'culture-fit' kind of dimensions during the hiring process. The second is (when a hiring decision has been made based on a large degree of fit; after all, there no 'perfect-fit') providing detailed feedback and coaching to the newly hired leader on those aspects/behaviors where there is insufficient fit. Not leveraging the wealth of data generated during the selection process for feedback and development/coaching is a costly miss that many organizations make.

Consider a bit of 'exorcism': When a leader works in an organization for a while, patterns of interaction develop around that leader. When that leader leaves the organization, a vacuum gets created and the patterns that were centred around that leader (or the 'ghost of that leader'; as Robert Pirsig says, ghosts are essentially such patterns) looks for someone to attach itself to and the new leader becomes the prime target. So, if the new leader is not careful, he/she gets sucked into those patterns and becomes part of the previous way of functioning before he/she realizes it. Now, especially if the leader has been hired with a mandate to drive change, this can seriously impair his ability to drive that change. Of course, all old patterns are not problematic and some of them might be even helpful. Continuing those helpful patterns can help the leader to provide the team some sense of continuity (and the assurance that the new leader doesn't disrespect the past), which is a big plus from the change management perspective. So, all that is required is to recognize the patterns and discontinue ('exorcise the ghost of') the dysfunctional patterns.

Being politically aware without 'playing politics': Driving change (which is often the reason why new leaders are brought in) is essentially a 'political' activity as it alters the current distribution of power. Even the very act of introducing a new leader into an organization, can change the power balance! Many leadership transitions fail because the new leaders could not recognize or manage the power dynamics. So, the requirement is to be sensitive to the political dynamics of the organization and to manage it without 'playing politics'. Yes, this is a tightrope walk (and sounds a bit mystical like 'doing without doing') that requires a very high level of self-awareness and critical self-monitoring. In a way, this is part of being 'enlightened'. Remember, enlightenment is about 'seeing things as they really are' (in the organization). Even for leaders who have been hired with a transformation mandate, 'it makes sense to understand something before trying to change it'!

Alignment, alignment, alignment: Soon after I joined one of my previous organizations (which had gone through multiple organization transformations) I asked a senior colleague what are the top three things that can make someone successful in that organization. His response was "alignment, alignment, alignment". I have seen this factor being relevant in other organizations also - especially for newly hired leaders. Having alignment with one's boss can be the starting point. My favourite question to ensure alignment on this is: "What would make you recommend the highest performance rating for me?". Enabling alignment with one's team through jointly developing the vision and way forward for the team is very powerful. Consulting widely with key stakeholders before one finalizes the vision and way forward is also very helpful (to deepen one's understanding of the organization, to clarify mutual expectations, to secure buy-in and to start building one's network). For a new leader it is very easy to make wrong (inappropriate) assumptions based on his experience in other organizations. So, these alignment conversations are most helpful. The principle of 'survival of the fittest' (that governs biological evolution) is applicable to the 'survival of newly hired leaders' also and we must remember that 'fittest' is defined in terms of 'being the best-adapted to the local environment'. Alignment is indeed a very powerful 'fitness' (fitness to the new organization) increasing activity!

So, where does this leave us? Bringing in new leaders is not some sort of a panacea for all the organizations' ills. Before bringing in new leaders, organizations should do some soul-searching on what exactly are the problems they are trying to solve and whether bringing in leaders from outside is the best option. The new leaders should bring in some capabilities or experiences that the organization doesn't have internally (and can't develop in the existing leaders within a reasonable time frame). 'Not being burdened by the past' shouldn't be the primary value that a new leader brings in. Else, the new leader would become part of the 'old' in a very short time (and becomes a candidate for replacing). Organizations should invest more in making the new leader successful. Apart from putting specific programs in place (like new leader integration, mentoring, coaching by senior leaders etc.), organizations should emphasize that the senior leaders who have hired the new leaders are accountable for making the new leaders successful.

Of course, the above discussion is applicable to all new hires and not just to new hires at senior leadership levels. It is just that possible negative impact of a failed or 'troubled' leadership transition (on the team and on the organization) is much higher. Leadership involves finding the right equilibrium between polarities, that too along multiple dimensions. Newly hired leaders need more help to find the appropriate equilibrium for the new organization context. The encouraging thing is that the upside of a successful leadership transition is also very high and hence worth the additional investment!

CHAPTER 10: PARADOXES IN LEAVING THE ORGANIZATION

Few men of action have been able to make a graceful exit at the appropriate time.

-Malcolm Muggeridge

When it comes to organizational life there are some moments that are more important than others from the employee experience and the employer employee relationship perspective. They are often referred to as 'moments of truth'. Exiting the organization is one such moment of truth. It can indeed be a very emotional moment for the employees. How well the exit is handled will have a huge impact on whether or not the employee becomes an ambassador for the company after the exit. From the employee point of view, the experience during the exit phase might determine how the employee remembers the overall employment experience with that company. Studies in Behavioral Economics have shown that what we remember about an experience could be very different from what we actually felt while we were going through the experience.

Let us look at some of the paradoxical aspects related to exiting an organization. We will begin by exploring what will be the ideal time to leave an organization. Often, there is a significant time lag between the employee deciding to leave an organization and the actual exit. We will take a closer look at this interesting phase and its implications. Attrition can significantly deplete the social capital of the organization. Social capital plays an important part in holding the organization together and in enabling it to function effectively. Hence, we will make an attempt to develop a more nuanced understanding of this aspect. After that, we will explore a very curious phenomenon – that of the sudden increase and decrease of the perceived value of the employee after he submits his resignation. These days, we often hear the statement that 'employees leave managers and not organizations. We will take a closer look at some of the paradoxical aspects of this point of view.

The paradox of the ideal time to leave

From the employee point of view, there two primary schools of thought here. The first is aligned to the philosophy that 'one should stop singing when the voice is still good'. This means that the employee should look for a job change when he/she is still doing well so that the employee will have sufficient time to find a better job and would be in a better position to negotiate with the new employer. The other point of view is aligned to the philosophy that 'grass is always greener on the other side'. This implies that 'all jobs look better from the outside' and that unless the employee is having serious difficulties that can't be addressed within the organization, he/she should not look for a change. Again, it means that unless the employee is very sure that he/she is going to get a much better deal, the employee shouldn't make a job change. The risk with this approach is that the employee might be forced to find a job in a very short period of time which will put him/her at a terrible disadvantage.

So, how do we resolve this? To me maintaining and enhancing one's employability is the key. There is merit in the advice that one should try to revise one's resume once in six months and if one is unable to make significant additions to the resume in two such cycles, one should look for a role change internally or externally. The other thing that the employee needs to consider is how the current organization he/she is working in looks at tenure in the organization. For example, does the organization look at a long tenure as a sign of 'solidity' and commitment or does it look at a long tenure as sign of rigidity and even that of the inability to find a good job? In organizations, that 'worship the new', that give the new employees a tremendous advantage over the tenured employees, it does make sense to figure out when is the transition from being a new employee to being an old-timer is likely to occur in the mind of the managers and leaders and proactively look out for a job when one is nearing that inflexion point. Yes, one should do all one can to validate that the new job offer is indeed better than what one already has.

In the valley of attrition

What exactly is this valley of attrition? An employee is said to be in the valley of attrition when the mind has left the organization, but the body is waiting for an offer letter to arrive!

While this concept might seem unorthodox or even a bit esoteric, this phenomenon is quite common in organizations. In employee engagement surveys, typically there is a question on the 'intention to leave' (for example, "Are you seriously considering leaving the organization?"). Now, if we compare the % of employees who answer in the affirmative to the question on 'intention to leave' with the actual 'attrition rate' we are likely to find a very significant gap (for example, 55% of the employees express the 'intention to leave' but the actual attrition is only 15% in a particular organization).

The gap (between the intention to leave % and the actual attrition %) indicates the % of employees who are 'stuck' or 'trapped' in the organization – they want to leave but can't find a job. This could be because they got so busy with their jobs that they didn't pay adequate attention to their employability (by developing market-relevant skills). This could be because they haven't developed job-hunting skills or because they are not sure if they can make a successful transition to another organization. This could also be because, while they want leave, they don't want to let go of some of the 'comforts' they have got used to in the current organization (and hence they are in the 'comfortably miserable' state). By the way, the first reason mentioned above, might give a hint for developing a 'sinister' employee retention strategy – making the employees less employable (or even unemployable) outside the current organization!

While there could be multiple reasons why people are trapped in their current jobs, it has important implications for employee happiness, employee engagement and the consequent business outcomes.

Feeling trapped is definitely not a pleasant state to be in! If you have never been in 'the valley of attrition' (and hence can't connect to this), imagine yourself having to wait for a long time in the departure lounge of an airport with your flight indefinitely delayed!

The trapped employees are unlikely be to be in the 'engaged' category (that is, putting in discretionary effort). They are likely to be in the 'not-engaged' or 'actively-disengaged' categories. These can lead to low performance and/or passive resistance! So, while the trapped employees are not 'attrition risks' they pose even greater dangers to the organization from performance and morale points of view! If some of these trapped employees have 'identity that is wrapped in their job', this could even lead to workplace violence!

It is a peculiarity of human nature that we are often clearer about what we don't want (I don't want to continue in this organization) as compared to what we really want (I want to join this particular organization)! The 'intention to leave' is somewhat similar to the 'flight' response in the 'fight or flight' basic repose to danger (or pain). This danger or pain can be psychological as well as well as physical. When we are running away from danger or pain, the main focus is to somehow get out of the current (dangerous/painful) situation and not really to get to a predefined better place. This can lead to sub-optimal career (job change) decisions especially in cases of 'intention to leave' triggered by specific events (for example, being overlooked for a promotion, disrespectful remark by the boss etc.). In the case of intention to leave created by more enduring factors (like lack of person-organization or person-job fit), the job changes are likely to be more thought-through/deliberate.

Social capital, restructuring and attrition

Social capital in an organization refers to the collective value of all social networks (connections among the individuals) in that organization. These connections have 'value' for both the organization and the employees.

A significant portion of the 'work' in organizations gets done through these connections (often referred to as the 'informal organization') rather than through the 'formal structure' in the organization. These 'connections' motivate employees to do things for one another beyond what is specified in the job descriptions. Hence social capital has a positive influence on productivity. The importance of social capital in the creation of intellectual capital has also been recognised. Since these 'connections' are difficult to copy, social capital could be a source of sustainable competitive advantage for the organization.

These 'connections' (social capital) could also help in addressing 'relatedness' needs of the employees. So, in addition to enabling the employees to get their work done faster/easier/better, these 'connections' contribute in meeting their social/'connectedness' needs. Thus, social capital could add to 'personal effectiveness at work' and the 'total employee deal' as perceived by the employees and hence it could have a positive influence on employee engagement and retention.

Organization restructuring is one of the popular ways of responding to a dynamic business environment. While the business case for restructuring is quite compelling in many contexts, the hidden costs of restructuring in terms of loss of social capital often gets overlooked. Restructuring breaks up the human networks/connections in organizations and dilutes the social capital in the organization. Since (as mentioned above) these connections are valuable for both the organization and the employees, there could be adverse impact on the organization (in the form of reduced productivity, reduction in the rate of intellectual capital creation, increased employee turnover/ attrition etc.) and on the employees (in terms of reduced engagement, work effectiveness, satisfaction etc.). Of course, many of these factors are interrelated and hence the adverse effects could get amplified.

As we have seen above, organization restructuring and the consequent loss of social capital could reduce the 'value' that the employees derive from organization and hence this could lead to employee turnover/attrition. The social networks bind the employees to one another and hence to the organization. It can also be said that one of the reasons that the employees don't want to leave an organization (to join another organization) is the reluctance to 'start all over again' (in terms of having to build new networks/

connections). Thus, if a restructuring breaks up their existing connections, employees might have less reason to stay on in an organization.

Costs of attrition like replacement cost and loss of productivity are well known. Apart from these costs attrition also leads to a further erosion in human capital as more social networks/connections get broken when employees leave. When 'key' employees (with a large number of strong connections) leave the impact on social capital would be more. It is also possible that employees might leave in groups if these groups have a large number of strong connections within them (especially if another organization offers an opportunity to maintain these connections).

Thus, one of the key hidden cost of restructuring could be in terms of loss of social capital and its ripple effects. Loss of connections/social capital could lead to attrition which in turn leads to a further erosion of social capital. This could lead to a vicious cycle and organizations should be careful about this. When an 'impact assessment' is done for the proposed restructuring exercise, the impact on social networks/connections/social capital should also be factored in. Since these social networks also serve as communication channels, the communication strategy for restructuring requires even more emphasis (as the restructuring could have broken up some of the existing communication channels). The overall change management plan should give specific attention to retain key people (people with a large number of strong connections) so as to reduce the erosion of social capital. The plan should also focus on creating an environment that would facilitate building of new connections to replace the old ones hence to restore and enhance the social capital in the organization.

The paradox of the sudden increase and decrease in value after resignation

There is an interesting (and unfortunate) pattern that repeats in many organizations. After an employee submits his resignation, the organization all of a sudden realizes how valuable is the employee to the organization and tries to communicate that to the employee in a compelling manner. If the employee refuses to stay in spite of all the persuasion, then the value of the employee suddenly drops and the employee might even be considered *persona non grata* with retrospective effect!

This pattern is unfortunate for many reasons. It is unreasonable to expect that the employees can read the mind of the organization. It can come as a surprise to the employee when told how valuable he/she was to the organization and what great plans the organization had prepared for her only after he/she the resignation. Often, employees have a more accurate idea on the possible risks for them in the organization than the possible opportunities. This happens mainly because the organization and the managers are often worried about raising expectations of the employees. It is indeed true that the organization and the managers should not make promises they can fulfil.

But this shouldn't mean that the employees won't know where exactly they stand and what are the possibilities open for them in the organization, So, the way out could be to communicate how the organization looks at the employee at this point and the actions that the organization intends to take subject to availability of opportunities and the relative readiness of the employee when those opportunities come up. Of course, the organization should also indicate the what help the organization would provide the employee to build readiness for target roles.

The second part of the phenomena (where an employee suddenly drops in perceived value after refusing to take back his resignation) results from attempt on the part of the leaders and managers to reduce cognitive dissonance. They think that if a good employee leaves that reflects poorly on the organization and the managers. So, if they can declare that the employee was not up to the mark all along, it does not come across as a loss to the organization. Of course, these kinds of actions destroy the trust of both the exiting employees and that of the other employees who watch this happen.

People leave managers not organizations?

'People leave managers and not organizations' is a very popular opinion these days. There is no doubt that the immediate supervisor is a key influencing factor in employee engagement and retention.

The problem happens when other factors that influence employee engagement and retention are ignored and the entire responsibility (or even blame) is put on the managers. Often there are other significant factors involved (for example, the basic nature of the job, 'Rewards' strategy, work environment, lack of career advancement opportunities etc.) over which first level managers don't have much influence. So, when the attrition level goes high, the tendency is to respond with 'training the managers on engaging and energising teams'.

This response also suits the senior leaders and HR admirably. The factors like basic nature of the job, 'Rewards' strategy, work environment, career advancement opportunities etc. are more difficult influence as compared to 'sending the poor managers for training'. While this gives leaders and HR the satisfaction of having 'responded quickly to the business challenge of attrition', unfortunately this does not solve the problem adequately. It also leaves the managers (who are already facing the consequences of attrition in their teams) more confused and frustrated. Hence, we come back to the point that 'system level issues' have to be addressed at the system level (and no amount of manager training can obviate this need).

There is another paradoxical aspect here. When a valuable employee submits his resignation should the manager and the organization try to convince the employee to stay back. If the employee stays back, it does help the manager and the organization, especially in the short run. However, it has been observed that many of these retained employees tend to leave after a few months. Also, if the organization gives salary hikes or promotions to retain the employees who submit their resignation it can be perceived as unfair by the remaining employees and also promote undesirable behaviors. Maybe, the best option is to proactively identify the employees that the organization must retain and take steps to ensure that they have no reason to look for opportunities outside the organization. Of course, this makes sense only if the organization has a good chance to be the career destination for the employee and not just a stepping stone or career enhancer.

CHAPTER 11: EMBRACING THE PARADOXES AND THE POSSIBILITIES

"The test of a first-rate intelligence is the ability to hold two opposed ideas in mind at the same time and still retain the ability to function".

-F. Scott Fitzgerald

We live in a world of contradictions. Paradoxical thinking enables us to deal with and even to embrace these contradictions. Yes, this calls for the willingness to live with the pain of cognitive dissonance that is will invariably result when we are making a deliberate effort to identify, appreciate and integrate the conflicting yet interdependent perspectives. However, the very act of recognising and wrestling with these contradictions opens up new possibilities for us.

Hence, our primary attempt in this book has been to take a closer look at the some of the key paradoxes, dilemmas and polarities that we encounter in business organizations, and, to wrestle with them for a while. This enables us to reach a higher level of awareness that makes it possible for us to respond creatively to the contradictions in our specific context. This helps us to actualize the possibilities for living a more fulfilling and effective life in business organizations. Hence, paradoxical thinking is not only about correctly identifying the paradoxes, but also about responding to them effectively.

As we have seen, the first step in paradoxical thinking is to develop a nuanced understanding of the paradoxical situation, the various options to respond to the situation, and the interdependencies and contradictions among those options. The next step is to explore the possibility of integrative solutions that reconcile these contradictions. In a way, this is similar to the process of resolving the tension between the thesis and the antithesis by finding a higher synthesis.

When such a synthesis is not possible, we try to achieve the right dynamic equilibrium between the competing forces and to constantly readjust the equilibrium point as the situation evolves. This could also involve switching between the options rapidly as per the demands of the situation while ensuring that the other considerations are also addressed at least at a threshold level. Here we are talking about micro-adjustments and not about swinging wildly between the positions. In a way, this is similar to riding a bicycle. A bicycle in motion is always tending to fall to one side or the other and we are constantly making micro-adjustments. Similar to what happened while we were learning to ride a bicycle, this gets progressively easy and then it becomes almost automatic.

Paradoxical nature is an inherent and crucial characteristic of life in organizations. However, we often overlook this aspect. This can lead to simplistic solutions that create more problems than they solve and do more harm than good. Creative tension and dynamic equilibrium between simultaneous opposites is required to maintain the vitality of the organizations and to avoid being driven to one set pattern or extreme. Hence, paradox is a necessary condition for organization effectiveness. Yes, thinking paradoxically might initially take the mind out of its comfort zone and make it think thoughts it does not want to think.

Paradoxes are divergent problems. While convergent problems should be broken into pieces and solved, divergent problems should be approached differently. They should be transcended using a higher awareness and scope. This often involves arriving at a higher plane where the diverging forces converge. While this is indeed more challenging, wresting with divergent problems often lead to breakthroughs. Creative leaps and integration are made possible by the presence of divergent problems and simultaneous opposites.

Without the ability to hold competing perspectives in mind simultaneously, we risk losing sight of the wisdom and opportunities that emerge when we pursue paradoxical thinking. Holding contradictory ideas in the mind is not easy, as it creates cognitive dissonance, stress and anxiety. However, it is a very valuable skill in a world full of contradictions.

While it is said that eastern cultures more naturally embrace opposites, it is indeed a learnable skill. It will also help us to resist the temptation to oversimplify the situation and to wish away the paradox. As organizations and individuals work though higher and higher levels of uncertainty and change, paradoxical thinking can enable us to differentiate ourselves.

Dealing with paradoxes need a high degree of openness, mental flexibility, intellectual honesty and humility. It also calls for some sort of ambidexterity and tolerance for ambiguity at the organizational level, to live with conflicting perspectives. This is what differentiates paradoxical thinking from the typical management approaches that worship clarity, predictability and control. A paradox cannot be solved in an algorithmic or prescriptive manner. If such a solution is attempted, it will create new problems and do more harm than good. This is the reason why many of the fundamental problems in management have not been 'permanently solved', even after decades of efforts by managers and consultants. However, if we approach them with the respect they deserve, paradoxes can reveal profound truths, spur creativity and help us to actualize the immense possibilities that come along with the inherent contradictions in organizational life!

This has been quite a journey that we have had through the wonderland of paradoxes and possibilities in organizational life. I hope that you have enjoyed this journey as much as I have enjoyed it. I will be honoured to hear from you regarding your encounters with the paradoxes, dilemmas and polarities in organizational life. Each of us are given a unique vantage point to look at life, and, by pooling our perspectives, we can definitely enrich the understanding of this important and challenging domain. You can reach me at prasad_kurian@yahoo.com

I wish you success in all your adventures with the paradoxes and possibilities in organizational life!

Prasad Kurian

Bangalore

January 2021